WRITE

Three Keys to Rise

YOUR

and Thrive as a

OWN

Badass Career Woman

STORY

Rebecca Fleetwood Hession

ISBN: 978-1-957723-00-6 (hard cover)
    978-1-957723-01-3 (soft cover)

Edited by: Erika Nein

Published by Warren Publishing
Charlotte, NC
www.warrenpublishing.net
Printed in the United States

To your dreams and your stories.

*May our collective courage to boldly write these stories
transform our lives and careers into a world we can't
wait to show our children and grandchildren.*

Your
Story
matters!

Love, Rebecca

In life, you'll be misunderstood. At some point, you'll be made out to be something you're not. When this happens, it's not as important to defend yourself as it is to know yourself. Know who you are, know what you mean, and know enough to feel secure even though you're not seen.[1]

—Kyle Creek, aka The Captain @sgrstk

PREFACE

Maybe you've had this conversation with yourself: *What's wrong with me? Why aren't I happy? I've got a great job, a family, a nice house … I should be grateful. So many people have it far worse. I need to suck it up and be grateful, be happy. Maybe I'll just buy a new journal and try harder to be grateful.*

Anyone? Just me?

That's our default: try harder.

If you're honest, though, some days you're done trying harder and you fantasize about running away to another country, living on the beach, and starting a hair-braiding business for tourists. You can picture it, you in that flowy floral maxi dress, barefoot, with sandy feet. Your hair is loosely knotted with those perfect little wisps that fall around your sun-kissed face. You're smiling, not the forced smile you use in meetings with shareholders and customers; it's the real smile that starts in your heart and spreads up to your face, your lips, your eyes. The smile that radiates out from your soul.

Then you wake up and realize you've got a family, the house, the dogs, all the things you'd have to deal with just to run away. Dammit, even running away feels hard. You snap out of the dream, push your hair out of your face, and open your laptop to tackle the next thing. First, you make a note on your task list.

1. Buy a new gratitude journal.

2. Get up at 5 a.m. instead of 5:30 so that you can be grateful.

We dig deeper, straighten our skirt, put our shoulders back, open the laptop, get back to work. The email, the meetings, the jerk in accounting, the PowerPoint presentation due Friday. Shit, did I forget a thing for the kids' school? Where is that form? Why can't schools use technology like the rest of the free world? Why is it all so hard? Truth be told, digging deeper isn't going to work much longer. We're getting to the bottom of that well that we've been pulling from for years.

Every night, a high achiever falls into bed exhausted from the day. But there are two kinds of tired. One is the tired that a nap or a few more hours of sleep won't fix. It's the tired that comes from *striving*, the tired that comes from not feeling valuable or relevant in your work and your life. Then there's the kind of tired where you fall into bed exhausted, and you don't dread the next day. Waking up ready to do it all again tomorrow because you know the value, relevance, and impact you have with other humans by the work you do. That's *thriving*.

I'm going to guide you there! Let me be your Thrive Guide.

Table of Contents

INTRODUCTION
Business Is Human

My earliest career memory is crawling under a house with my grandfather. He was a plumber. I was a plumber's helper. The great thing about being a ten-year-old plumber's helper is the ease with which you can crawl in and out of tight spaces. We'd go in and he'd diagnose and send me back to the truck for the tools he needed. There's something so powerful about being valuable. For all I know, he was sending me to the truck so I'd stop talking in his ear while he worked, but in my young mind, I mattered.

This is when I became passionate about work. The feeling of being valuable and relevant continued to grow from there. I used to think it was just about my work ethic or discipline of my checklist and plans, but it's far more. Our jobs aren't something we do just for the paycheck; they're a part of us, a part of our purpose.

Over the next thirty years, I acquired mountains of experience and education, none of which I ever could have imagined as that ten-year-old plumber's helper surrounded by swearing and toolboxes. A small-town girl living in a trailer on her grandfather's farm didn't know there was such a thing as sharing the stage with the world's thought leaders, contributing to best-selling books, or being a consultant to smart, talented executives in corporate America. She had only her feelings, and feeling valuable was good; she wanted more of that.

Thirty years later, with a truckload of glass awards stored in a box under the stairs, an abundance of shining accolades, and unending expectations, I found myself home for two months with pneumonia, wondering, questioning, and reflecting. I was conflicted. By all standards, my life was a shining success worthy of my awards and recognition. I lived on a twenty-three-acre estate with two lakes, a big house I designed, two kids, two dogs, and a husband. The American dream. Sure, I was sick, and that was a bummer. But being sick holed up in your Barbie mansion is a first-world problem.

Success didn't necessarily "feel" like what I thought it would. I had this ache for something more—and it wasn't more meetings. I was a top performer. I knew all the buzzwords, the corporate speak, and the productivity techniques. I could teach you all of my best practices for selling $35 million and lead classes on innovation in global consulting, but what I didn't know was how I *felt*. I'm not talking about the pneumonia pains in my chest; this was a different kind of deep ache. From the outside, my life looked like a fairy tale. But I wasn't sure how I felt about my life, about who I was, and who I wanted to be. I was aching for more meaning, but I discovered that the answer wasn't "out there." The answer came from within.

At some point, I realized what I needed and what my business required were very different. Business is human. We are humans serving humans with products and services in exchange for currency. I was a business consultant, a sales professional, steeped in profit and loss, productivity gains, and investment return. I knew how to control, measure, and optimize a business like a boss! I had the awards and the paycheck to prove it. What I had lost track of were my human needs. What did I really want? Who really knew me? Would I be loved and accepted if I wasn't number ten on the global sales report? Whom was I serving? Was I serving other humans or the machine of the business?

The more I allowed myself to reflect, the more I craved to know more. I wasn't sure who I was anymore. Without the distraction of my striving life, a pain and a longing began to bubble to the surface.

- Was I happy?
- When had I been truly happy?
- What would I be doing if I wasn't so damn busy all the time?
- What were my dreams? Did they still matter?
- Had I allowed my house and my things to be enough? Had *stuff* replaced my dreams?
- Had I accomplished anything meaningful?
- What was the cause of so much stress and anger in my life?
- What did I really want?
- And, most troubling, who really knew me? Who knew the real me?

Know Thyself First

The deepest human need is to be seen, heard, and known. How would I fulfill this need without discovering and knowing myself first? I wasn't sure who I was anymore; how could I expect others to see me and know me?

I spent the next several weeks studying me and my story as if it were my job. Because it was. Feelings began to surface as I stripped away the years of busyness, like wallpaper in an old Victorian, each layer from my past. I scraped and peeled and looked for what was underneath. There were beautiful memories and dreams and also dark and angry parts of my story. There were emotions I wasn't sure I was ready to explore. There was loneliness, so much loneliness. I was scraping away more achievement, more acreage, granite countertops, awards, more money, broken relationships, meaningful relationships, layer by layer, to find the real me underneath it all.

I realized I had been treating my entire life like a business, trying to control, measure, and optimize my time, my relationships, and my achievements. I knew this would never give me satisfaction. I would never meet my human needs with business practices. What I craved were primal human needs to be personal, emotional, and social. To see and be seen. To feel and navigate back to my gifts, talents, and dreams buried deep at the bottom of my heart, where the love lives. Buried under striving and achievement.

I would later learn that the real question was: Could I still have a rewarding career full of success, awards, and achievements *and* meet my personal needs? They seemed so jumbled together; I wasn't sure what was what and who was who.

Still too sick to put on my "I can fix this" superhero outfit, I was left to just look inside and be honest about what I saw. I wanted to believe my life was better than what I was feeling; was I really this lonely and empty? I went for evidence—my stack of journals tucked in a bedside table.

That day, I was slowly feeling better and had showered, one of my new markers of accomplishment. The energy to shower and dry my hair felt heroic. I was also grateful for the time to rest. I couldn't remember a time I had rested like that. To just be. With a Midwest winter in full swing, I was wrapped in white, a sign I would later see as a cleansing. I gathered my terry robe close and sank into my white chair to take in the snowy scene outside. The sun was sneaking through the windows, inviting me to be courageous and explore more of my story, to see it fully in the light.

For the next five hours, while my kids were at school, I read each of my journals back to back. Year after year, the story of me unfolded. There were hopes, dreams, and struggle. Disappointment and despair were followed by a profound period of "suck it up." There were pages and pages of the same: my story unfolding, then getting stuck. Each year the suck it up proportion was more profound and the hopes and dreams less pronounced. Profound loneliness cried out on those pages. I saw my dreams neglected and then abandoned, lost to my striving for achievement to meet the business's needs and everyone else's needs.

A glass award for top sales where the writer used to be, the hardwood floors and stunning estate where the love and comfort were supposed to live.

I knew this was my story. I saw my handwriting on each of the pages. And yet, I saw less and less of the real me in each of the journals as I finished them and they landed on the floor beside me. The same narrative, lived over and over like the movie *Groundhog Day*. I saw my name as the main character, yet it felt like someone else had been playing the part. Only shadows of me were left; my hopes and dreams were tucked away like fine china, used only on special occasions but disregarded most days. The character in the story I was reading sounded more robotic and machine-like than human: busy, cranking and churning, producing. This was not the story I imagined for myself.

I'd worked harder and harder each year, the effort proven in those pages. The more I achieved, the harder I worked and the less I recognized me. The people in my story loved me but didn't know me; they needed me and they needed my achievements. They applauded me but couldn't see me. I was hidden, and no one was coming to save me. There's no one jumping in to save the high achiever, no prince on a white horse, no distress ever shown from the damsel. Who was coming to save me?

If you search how to save someone who's drowning, the first advice you'll see is usually: *Don't expect a casualty to be shouting for help; they might be struggling to breathe. Drowning looks very different in the movies. If you're not sure, ask if they need help. If they say yes or don't answer at all, it's time to act.*

I was drowning. I wouldn't answer at all. It was entirely up to me to save me, guided by my God-given inner knowing and the courage to initiate change.

I closed the last page in my stack of journals. I gathered my robe tighter, shivering. I sank deeper in my chair and looked out into the blanket of fresh snow. This was the blinding light sent to save me, the sign of a new beginning, a fresh white page. God was showing me my story and throwing me a lifeline, impelling me to write new chapters.

I didn't know what the next chapters would look like. I only knew it was time to flip the script. It was time to go on an adventure to find myself, reclaim me. I knew there would be challenges, that I would struggle changing my story, but I wanted to play my role in life authentically. Whatever effort it took, *I* was coming back. I would breathe again. Thriving, not striving. I didn't want just *things* and a great paycheck; I wanted to live and work fully from my soul. I was ready to write my own story like a great book or movie, a story with emotion, heroes, villains, and an epic adventure. Our lives aren't meant to be a business textbook and list of accomplishments; our stories are unique to us, emotional and engaging. That day, I committed to rediscovering myself and the soulful nature of being human.

What is *soul?* I first had to ask myself that question. I needed to peel back the material things in my life and go deeper into those emotional, spiritual, and moral connections. *Soul* is what makes you … you.

We discover more and more about ourselves throughout life's journey. We find clues day by day that speak to and define our soul and connect us to those we need and those who need us. This exploration is our life's work, where we learn about what speaks to our soul and how our soul speaks to others. Our lives and businesses can be soulful when done with intention and a focus on thriving, not striving.

The difference between *striving* and *thriving* may sound slight or a fancy play on words. I promise you the difference is profound. Your brain is designed to seek thriving. Every day that we wake up, our brain has one job, to be sure we survive and thrive. Unfortunately, somewhere between surviving and thriving, people get stuck striving. Striving is writing a manual or a textbook; thriving is writing a story.

Striving actually means there's opposition that requires us to battle and struggle. To strive is to battle for our worth by controlling, measuring, and optimizing our human life like it's being produced on a factory assembly line.

Thriving is an active pursuit to grow, prosper, and flourish, rooted in neuroscience, nature, and the Holy Spirit. It is developing your career from the inside out, guided by your inner knowledge of who you are, not searching out there for the answer in what you do. To thrive in your profession is to honor your human needs to be personal, emotional, and social. You can honor your human needs *and* serve the business's needs to control, measure, and optimize. The secret is not confusing the two but knowing how to honor both. Honoring your human needs is to be seen, heard, and known for your unique story and serving others by being valuable, relevant, and impactful. We don't search for our meaning; we discover it.

Business Is Human	
Business Needs	**Human Needs**
Control	Personal
Measure	Emotional
Optimize	Social

CHAPTER 1
Striving vs. Thriving

Hey, are you still searching? Are you still buying all the books, watching TED Talks late at night, maybe considering another degree, continually looking for the answers? I get it. I spent decades searching too. You know the stance, hunched over something, maniacally searching? Like a scientist peering through a microscope looking for something too small to see with the human eye, believing there's something there we just can't see? Searching for the answer to feel better about your life and career? Looking for more meaning, not more meetings?

Searching outside of ourselves for meaning is striving.

Girl, stand up. Stop searching, stop hovering, stop studying. Go to the mirror or pull out your phone and open your camera; look at your reflection. I don't mean leaning in, looking at the wrinkles or turning sideways at what sticks out or sags. Muster the love and kindness you reserve for your kids or your dog. Now, look into your eyes and your heart. Do you see that? That's everything you need to thrive in your life and business. You already possess it; it's within you. Right now, you have it—the answers, the strength, and the potential. We can and should meet these human emotional needs through our work.

Yes, our work is work, with goals, metrics, and so many damn meetings. But the very best companies and leaders bring their humanity into work and acknowledge the human needs in each other. They build the business to serve humans.

It's time to explore your humanity through a new mindset that will allow you to create the life you desire. It's time to shed the expectations and societal norms that keep us struggling, striving, and stuck.

Release some of your limiting beliefs. Let go of the idea that your career is a separate thing from the rest of your life. You know that elusive work-life balance thing you've been searching for? Life and career are not separate things to be balanced. That's a bullshit lie meant to sell you books. My career is as much a part of my life as my kids, my dogs, my parents. My meaning and purpose is being discovered through my work.

Your career is a part of your story. You are not a work human and a personal life human; you are one human. Business is human.

There are four ways to identify striving:

1. If money and financial needs trump your unique personal needs or story
2. If there is a need to control, causing a loss of human connection in your life and work
3. If you identify success with your title, your industry, or your paycheck
4. If you fail to recognize a common cause to work together to achieve

The History of Striving

A life of striving is an innocent mistake. We started our adult lives focused on survival: pay the rent, pay off the student loans. And we did. We did it so well. We got promoted, and things were more comfortable financially; we planned some fun vacations, bought a new car. So proud, we continued to acquire and obtain. Our first miss in the journey from surviving to thriving was believing money came first. When that didn't work to find meaning, we tried adding more. We added kids, a mortgage, a seat on a nonprofit, and volunteering at church; we volunteered to plan the family reunion. More and more and more ... boom, striving snuck in like a thief in the night. It slid its key into the door of our four-bedroom in the suburbs, bellied up to our granite countertops, and poured itself a nice cabernet. And slowly, it began to rob our joy, our satisfaction, and our well-being.

Strive, angry and bitter, told us to work harder, get up earlier, add a yoga class, buy a new journal, go back to school. Make sure we've got it together. Strive tells us more is better, less is slacking, and rest is for the weak. Strive taps you on the shoulder on Sunday night and says, "By the way, have you seen your week? Better get to it, or you'll never get caught up." And it wasn't just us; this was the societal norm we stepped into.

It's time to escort strive to the door with a swift kick in the ass.

Getting to this place of striving and burnout didn't happen overnight. Let's take a trip in our "wayback machine" to see how business has evolved over the last five to six decades. Let's take a peek back into the 1700s and earlier, into the life of a farming society; the overall common cause was survival. Everyone knew their place in providing for each other. Whether it was plowing fields, spinning yarn into fabric for clothes, or diagnosing medical care and using herbs they grew for treatment, a community of humans worked together for a common cause. If you didn't plow and plant, many people you loved didn't eat or survive. If you couldn't diagnose ailments, people would likely die. Your life and work mattered to another human.

Then came the industrial revolution with the introduction of machining, tools, and factories.[2] Factories break down the work into departments, each department to be controlled, measured, and optimized with the goal for the company to be better collectively with each department in charge of its production and quality control. The fundamental purpose of the industrial revolution was financial. The belief was that if we could increase our economic environment and move past survival, we'd enjoy greater quality of life. In many ways that was true.

But, in a grossly misunderstood and unintended consequence that wouldn't play out for decades, we lost much of the human connection that surviving together gave us in a farm-based society. If you didn't show up for work in the industrial age, you didn't get paid. You had a personal consequence, but you didn't feel the community consequence of missing work. If you didn't show up to do your work in an agrarian society, people died; you knew how and why you mattered.

As humans, we're wired to survive and thrive; this transition to the industrial age model of life and work introduced striving.

1. We started to lose the human connection of business. Today, our work is mostly still industrial, made of pieces and parts, departments, and business units without a collective human story that ties the components together personally, emotionally, and socially.

2. We fell in love with control. The industrial age did create a boom in economic security. Because controlling, measuring, and optimizing our work gave us such financial benefit in our lives, we started believing we should control all aspects of our human lives.

3. We put money before our human needs and stories.

Since separating work into various departments worked so well in the factory, the same structure was applied to education. Today's school model hasn't changed much since the early 1900s. Topics are separated like parts on an assembly line with no context for how those topics fit together in life outside of school. No clarity, no context, no human connection for the story. You can excel in math, fail in English, and the combined average called your GPA says you're just that, "average." And this education system does little to show you how any of it relates outside of school in the years to come called the rest of your life. You can strive to succeed at school and have no understanding of the context and connection to make your algebra grade meaningful to your life as a mom, a graphic designer, or a CEO. You can succeed at school and have no idea what that means for *you*.

Focus is placed on the system with a high value of standardization and no value on each human student's uniqueness. You can graduate with a 4.0 and fail at life. You can be the school dropout and change the world like Frank Lloyd Wright or Steve Jobs.

After twelve years on an assembly line of education, we earned the right to pay handsomely for another four years if we wanted to truly strive for success. Is it any wonder that between school and work, we take this factory model of obedience and standardization as Holy Writ? Have we seen or known anything different after being obedient, being told what is right and what is wrong, with little to no understanding of how to honor our uniqueness and connection as humans?

In Seth Godin's manifesto *Stop Stealing Dreams*, he writes:

> A hundred and fifty years ago, adults were incensed about child labor. Low-wage kids were taking jobs away from hard-working adults. Sure, there was some moral outrage about seven-year-olds losing fingers and being abused at work, but the economic rationale was paramount. Factory owners insisted that losing child workers would be catastrophic to their industries and fought hard to keep the kids at work—they said they couldn't afford to hire adults. It wasn't until 1918 that nationwide compulsory education was in place.
>
> Part of the rationale used to sell this major transformation to industrialists was the idea that educated kids would actually become more compliant and productive workers. Our current system of teaching kids to sit in straight rows and obey instructions isn't a coincidence—it was an investment in our economic future. The plan: trade short-term child-labor wages for longer-term productivity by giving kids a head start in doing what they're told.

Large-scale education was not developed to motivate kids or to create scholars. It was invented to churn out adults who worked well within the system. Scale was more important than quality, just as it was for most industrialists.[3]

Our education system does very little to honor our uniqueness or the exploration of our thoughts, feelings, ideas, or talents. School is factory-built for efficiency, not for human needs. School doesn't give two shits about your unique needs. Ask any parent with a child who doesn't learn well in a traditional classroom. School is a business focused on controlling outcomes to ensure funding, a money-first system, especially higher education when you're actually paying real money, not those hidden tax dollars, for the classes. Guess how much more money they make for a five-year student versus a four-year student?

And for those students with a biological tendency toward greater empathy and sensitivity to others, this factory of compliance and obedience does very little to nurture intuition and sense of self. In the factory model of education, individual achievement is the goal; in fact, in the classroom, helping is cheating. So now here we are, grown-ass adults wondering who we are, why we don't feel as fulfilled as we thought by our success and achievements.

We worked so hard to get it right. We worked hard to meet their expectations. Sometimes we even stop listening to our own hearts and desires to please the system. When we live our lives as we think we're "supposed to" instead of who we really are, we won't derive a sense of satisfaction about our work, even if we've received all the awards and a huge paycheck.

This is the root of striving.

When the factory mindset—the quest to control, measure, and optimize—began to increase the economy, we began to believe money comes first. Our human needs have been striving and battling the business needs ever since, landing us in this place of burnout. And here we are not knowing ourselves very well and with a lot of money that won't buy us thriving or joy, just some fleeting happiness that we need to keep achieving to keep buying, always scratching the wrong itch.

I bring this to light so you're not too hard on yourself. We were taught striving from nearly our beginning, kindergarten, just five years into our life on this earth. The factory mentality spilled over into our schools, our homes, our parenting, our wellness, our youth sports; it's taken over our human lives. And now the factory system we've created for business never shuts down. We're global, 24/7.

It's so pervasive and accepted that it doesn't even get acknowledged that it's hurting us. We didn't notice that we were losing bits of our humanity along the way. Our lives became little factories focused on producing work, grades, promotions, achievements, and degrees. We've normalized an addiction to time, control, and achievement-based success, the need for our accomplishments to be validated from somewhere or someone outside of ourselves. A quest to obtain the answer to a great life from somewhere "out there."

We've been in the hustle-and-grind factory system of business for so long that we've lulled ourselves into believing this is normal. Have you ever worked hard to achieve something, and once you reached it there wasn't nearly the sense of fulfillment you anticipated? The award, the promotion, the bigger house actually left you feeling exhausted and a little less, not the "more" you were hoping for? Achievements and rewards are outstanding to celebrate success, but the emotional gain is fleeting, so we set our sights on another thing to achieve. We're looking for ways to fill the human void with things, but the only way to honestly fill the gap is with human connection.

Working habitually and mindlessly without emotion, like factory assembly work, is like waiting for the quality-control inspector to stamp us APPROVED, GRADE A, or CERTIFIED and often fearing we might be stamped REJECT or DEFECT by the lack of measured output in our lives. Hardly inspiring, this is striving.

We now have an achievement-based culture steeped in competition, comparison, and external validation of our worth. We believe we're supposed to control humans. This goes against our essential needs as humans to be ourselves and live in a social community working together to serve one another. We've neglected these needs for so long that we've arrived in this crisis of burnout in business but also a decline in the mental health of ourselves and our children. I often think the days of the one-room schoolhouse with an education gained through helping, sharing, and communication is the better approach—you know, an education that is more personal, emotional, and social.

There's no satisfaction, let alone well-being, in fighting a battle each day. Striving brings stress and exhaustion. It carries a healthy dose of isolation and loneliness too. Striving buries our human needs under a pile of busy tasks where no one ever sounds the bell for our break.

Business has become the enemy, and it doesn't have to be that way. We don't have to strive against our business needs to meet our human needs. Our sense of worth and value as a human doesn't have to be at the mercy of our jobs and our achievements. What if instead of seeing careers and business as a destination we seek, we can instead see business as the opportunity to explore our interests, explore the value we can provide? Our sense of worth and value as a human can be the powerful motivator for our career and how we serve in our community. We can flip the script to honor and value our personal human needs first and use them to serve other humans in our business. This is thriving.

So, don't quit your job and move to Tahiti; there's a better way. We need you as a high achiever in this world of work. We need you to build things, lead people, and be a part of our economy. We need you. We can rally together and do this differently.

The answer isn't more; the answer isn't out there. The answer isn't in control or in comparison.

It's time to rise up and out of the rubble of striving and conflict.

It's time to grow, prosper, and flourish.

It's time to thrive.

Let's explore how we've neglected the most powerful force in our life and our business, our human needs and our human gifts. Let's tap into the power of our humanity with our built-in desire to help and serve, to be valuable and relevant like the intuitive guidance I received as a plumber's helper.

We can have the business success we desire when we lead with our human needs. This gives us an infinite capacity to grow personally and professionally. When we take responsibility for our human needs first and lead teams and companies with this same guidance and expectation, we have an infinite capacity for growth. It's time to start the age of humanity.

I feel your sense of urgency, striving for a checklist to figure out how to get some of this *now*! This is part of the challenge. We can't manufacture a life of thriving; we're humans, not machines. We can't buy thriving, but we can create the conditions for thriving by tapping into our needs and desires. Thriving is more like planting a garden, choosing the right plants for our weather and soil. We create the conditions to thrive by honoring our human needs to be personal, emotional, and social and then taking our humanity to work where we control, measure, and optimize our business strategies to have value, relevance, and impact to other humans.

Ready for Change? Intentional vs. Habitual

During my pneumonia-induced time of reflection, it was painfully apparent I needed change. Yet, I didn't treat this as a "Life Project 101: Rebecca changes by end of the fiscal year." People who think they know me assume this is how I would address change. I've been the business guru, the lover of all things goals and execution. The truth is, I had already spent way too much time trying to take my gut instincts and innate talents and put them into corporate speak and strategic plans to validate I was smart. This belief that everything needed a strategic plan is what got me into this situation. Instead, I became more intentional and less habitual. I let myself notice more, feel more, explore more, be more human.

In the months and years following pneumonia, I set out to write the next chapters of my story, not just acquire more achievements. To begin intentionally writing the story I wanted to live in, I had to question everything about my feelings and how I spent my days.

I had been living in habits of hustle and grind for decades, striving to meet everyone's expectations. I like to work and I brought amazing results to my company; therefore, I was rewarded. My accomplishments and my big paycheck afforded us many vacations and a big house on an estate property. But I was on the hustle and grind assembly line. *Keep cranking it out; if you slow down, you'll let people down, you'll stop achieving, you'll get behind.*

Habits evoke a sense of autopilot, something you do mindlessly. Habits have the reputation of being replicable. *If it's good for you, it should be good for me.* This is true when it comes to brushing your teeth and using your turn signal. Choices about your story, your career, and your relationships, however, should be made intentionally, not habitually. I never again want to live my life mindlessly or try to copy the success of another.

I began asking myself *what was my intent* versus *what do I want to get done?* I wanted to live more authentically from my dreams and desires and to do so with authentic relationships composed of people that truly knew me and weren't just interested in what I could produce. I was overwhelmed by how much change I needed and wanted. I craved real human connection. I wanted real conversations to share my hopes, dreams, and desires. I wanted to share my fears and frustrations without the expectation I would have answers—or if I didn't have the answers something must be wrong with me, that I'd lost my edge. I wanted to explore, trip, fall, get back up, and try again. I wanted life to be messier, a beautiful messy adventure living with more curiosity and courage. More trying shit out, less "get it right."

On our treadmill of tasks and frenetic activity, the quest to get more done and arrive at the illusive space of "caught up" is striving, a battle against time and task. Intentional, however, gives you a variety of options and autonomy. You can intentionally cultivate love and joy or bitterness and contempt; the choice is entirely up to you. Living with intention allows an ebb, a flow, and a rhythm more in keeping with our human story. Living with intention honors all of the emotions, the struggles, and the humanity.

As I began to plan for the changes I would make in my life, I was reminded of an article Alan Deutschman wrote for *Fast Company* magazine, one I had quoted many times when working with clients orchestrating organizational change. The lessons in this article became a foundation for the changes that were about to take place in my life.

The title "Change or Die" seemed fitting based on how I was feeling after two months of pneumonia and reading through the life I no longer wanted to live. The article reveals the stunning choices made by cardiology patients who had undergone a traumatic and expensive bypass surgery. The patients could have prevented additional surgery or death by making changes to their lifestyle, including food and exercise choices. Yet, two years after surgery only 10 percent had made the necessary changes to prevent further heart problems—10 percent![4]

For these cardiac patients, facts and figures didn't evoke change, nor did the fear of dying. Fear of dying changed only short-term behaviors. The 10 percent with long-term changes had painted a picture of the joyful life they wanted to live, not the fear of dying.

This illustration affirms our need to start with a story when contemplating any change. Our brains process information as a story. Data and facts do little to sustainably change our behavior. Emotions are the keys to unlocking lasting change. Yup, emotions. Not just any emotions—we're talking positive, joy-filled emotions. So much for those facts, figures, charts, and graphs you prepared for your last meeting. Nope, not all that helpful. Bring the graphs and charts to illustrate your story, not to stand on their own. Turns out, bringing the love and the light is a special ingredient for getting the changes we want in life and business. You know why? We're humans, not machines.

Writing an emotional, joyful story is the start to a thriving life and business. What is the story you are writing for your life? Howard Gardner, a professor at Harvard's Graduate School of Education, has looked at what works most effectively for heads of state and corporate CEOs. "When one is addressing a diverse or heterogeneous audience," he said, "the story must be simple, easy to identify with, emotionally resonant, and evocative of positive experiences."[5] Shouldn't all of our endeavors in business prepare us to address a diverse and heterogeneous audience? As humans, we are each unique in our gifts, talents, abilities, and experiences—making us diverse in character and content. Let me translate Gardner's corporate speak: if you want to live a thriving life and to lead a thriving company full of growth and prosperity, intentionally write a simple, joyful story.

Another characteristic of the cardiology patients who made successful lifestyle changes? They had support. We're wired for connection and belonging, story to story, human to human. Our human stories are meant to serve others. Thriving is a human condition meant to use our differences to derive joy and well-being in helping and supporting one another. When seeking change, find your joy, write your story and reach out to serve another.

As I looked at my life, what gave me the most joy was my value, relevance, and impact to other people, not my achievements. The awards I received often made me uncomfortable, exacerbating the fear of not hitting my goals the following year, unable to keep up the constant expectation of producing.

I wanted a life surrounded by people who really knew me, not just who knew what I could accomplish. I didn't need perfection; I needed connection, to help and be helped, to feel the connection from my clients, friends, and family—that was life-giving. So I made many significant changes in my life.

Over four years, I divorced, sold our big home and moved, shook up the friend group, and made a career change. Like unraveling a tangled skein of yarn, I worked on one knot at a time. On my last day of a nineteen-year career, there I was, sitting alone in my home office. I had been a remote worker all of my career, so that was nothing new. But this day was very different. At 6 p.m., I looked through my files one last time to be sure I had transferred all of my personal info. After nineteen years, your work computer becomes personal and stores your daughter's prom pictures and the documents from the sale of your house. I was uneasy in closing out the day, hoping I hadn't left something important hostage to a login that would no longer be mine. It was unnerving. I realized how intertwined work and life really were. Finally, I closed my laptop. *Click.*

The quiet loudly filled the room. I sat looking out the window with a cocktail of emotions leaving me dizzy and confused. This was how it ends? A career lasting longer than both of my marriages ends with the echoing click of a closing laptop in an empty room? Where was the parade? Maybe some balloons? Why hadn't the CEO called me on this momentous occasion? I had given my life to this company. Traveled on days I should have been helping with school plays, mustered the courage to make many difficult calls and decisions. I sold $35 million for this company! This was really how it would end?

Truth be told, I had provided six months' notice and was given many accolades and beautiful messages of goodbye. Several leaders asked me to stay. Yet, the emotions were confusing. If I'm honest, I was a little pissed, bitter, and frustrated. That's what humans do; we have emotions about our work. Our work is personal, emotional, and social. I did what many badass women do when feeling dissed and pissed. I bellied up to my kitchen counter and poured a very tall glass of cabernet and nursed my sour grapes.

A few sips in, prepared to go down the woe-is-me, this-is-bullshit tirade, I had a little talk with myself. *Come on Rebecca, you chose to leave. You had six months of goodbyes and thank-yous and please-don't-leave-we'll-give-you-whatever-you-wants. All. The. Things.*

I was leaving to venture out on this "free to be me," sexy entrepreneurial journey I'd craved for so long. Why did it feel so confusing? So lonely?

The truth is, I wasn't sure who I was without a well-known company logo to lean on. I wasn't sure who I was without dropping my name among the famous authors I worked with. I wasn't sure who I was without an expense account and planning the next reward trip to party with my people and bask under the palm trees of sales success. How would I introduce myself? How would I know if I was good?

This was sobering. More cabernet, please.

Because one of my best traits is annoying levels of optimism, I looked for the lesson in these emotions. Our emotions are valuable teachers when we honor them. I want to feel all of the feelings, explore them as guides.

There it was, sitting beside me at the kitchen counter: the truth. I was the exact same person who earned those glass sales awards. I was the exact same person who went on all the trips for top sales. I was the exact same person with clients who loved and cared for me. I possessed all the same gifts, talents, and abilities sitting there "wining/whining" at my counter. It was now up to me to use those gifts, talents, and abilities differently. My story hadn't ended; it was time to write a new chapter. The lesson I would pick up and write in my journal that day: *Always know your worth. It's something we hold within us; it's not something we acquire. It's not something a company can take away or reward. I can go and become anything I want. I hold my worth in my skills, my heart, my soul, and my mind. As long as I can utilize my unique talents, I have value. I will continue to seek opportunities to use my gifts to be valuable, relevant, and impactful.*

Here's the takeaway: when we know ourselves well and can stand tall in our own stories, we can choose to leave and make changes confidently. Humans move in and out of companies; we don't expect companies to make us more or less human. We're not a hostage to a company shift in strategy. When we expect our companies and careers to cater to our every need to feel valued, we set ourselves up for disappointment and disillusionment. No matter how valuable you are to a company, when you leave, it replaces you. That's the deal. When we tie our value and relevance so tightly to a company, a brand, or a job title, we're striving; we're in a battle to stay attached to that system.

But when we know our value, we can confidently carry that into the next chapter of our story, thriving and growing, ready for the next opportunity. When we know ourselves well, we gain courage and confidence. That's what I want for each of you reading this book. I want you to know yourselves so well that you'll never allow yourself to strive again. You won't be at the mercy of a title or an achievement to validate your worth. You'll explore the things in your heart, the dreams God has planted in you. You'll build a career from your soul.

I'm ready to be your Thrive Guide and help you write your thrive story. I'm ready to help you create the conditions to thrive in life and business. I'm here to hold up the mirror for reflection and help you see you. Thriving is a personal endeavor. The answer is within you, pen in hand, as writer of your story.

As your Thrive Guide, I'll give you the three keys to create the conditions to thrive: story, money, and rhythm. These keys open the door to **growth**, **prosperity**, and a **flourishing** life—the very definition of thrive.

Thriving is an active and intentional pursuit to create the conditions for us to *grow* like a well-tended garden. It is not a respite from the frenetic pace of our striving life. This isn't taking a break; it's shifting your mindset and focus on leading with your humanity as your career advantage. It's going from the idea of acquiring more validation and more degrees and contorting your life to fit some production schedule, to using your work to add value, have impact, and be relevant to other humans. The focus is on who you are first, then on what and how you do it.

And yes, *prosper* means to be paid well and to know our worth; there's absolutely no shame in that game. Prosper with money, joy, and happiness. I'm not some airy-fairy money-doesn't-matter type with no concern for the bottom line. In fact, a robust bottom line fuels our ability to do great work and serve more of our fellow humans. I love big bottom lines, and I cannot lie.

When we flourish, we grow or develop in a healthy or vigorous way, primarily due to a particularly favorable environment. Work and career have the ability to heal, not hurt; they can be a part of our love for life, not something we endure to pay the bills.

Are you ready for a change? Are you prepared to put down striving ways and see things differently? Are you prepared to do things differently to be relevant, add value, and create a ripple effect of impact into the future?

Take a deep breath, let your shoulders relax, extend your hand, and let me give you those keys. I want you to feel the freedom of open doors, beautiful relationships, and a rewarding career. It will be up to you to use these keys to open your doors.

CHAPTER 2
The Three Keys to Thriving

Here are your three keys, and the order matters.

Key #1 is story, and it unlocks the door to growth.

Key #2 is money, and it unlocks the door to prosperity.

Key #3 is rhythm, and it unlocks the door to flourishing.

Story

We start with *story* to learn to trust ourselves, to build a life based on our intuition, the collection of our lifetime of experiences and inner knowing. Writing our own story builds trust and confidence in ourselves. The more we trust ourselves, the more we can courageously explore opportunities to enrich our lives without reliance on societal expectations and comparison of success.

Our story is constantly evolving, chapter by chapter. Being intentional about writing our story unleashes infinite growth and possibility. Writing our own story includes self-care, self-esteem, confidence, courage, intuition, our connections, our communication, predominantly the way we speak to ourselves. Our story is the beautiful culmination of our past, present, and the dreams of our future. It's the stirring combination of our struggles and our deep, burning desires. The key to our growth lies within us. We don't go out and search for it; we unlock it from deep within us through the power of knowing and sharing our story.

Writing our own story brings out our natural and innate development to change physically, emotionally, and socially as we progress and mature. The etymology of the word *grow* is rooted in botany. Our personal growth, much like our lawn, requires creating the right conditions. Could we put the same intentional effort into our personal growth that we do for our lawn or our garden? Do we know the conditions we need to grow? Each of us has specific conditions to fuel our growth.

Money

Money is a necessary and neutral commodity. Life requires money. All careers are based on a money-making model for the business. Money is neutral; it isn't good or bad. It's the story we place on money that makes it good or bad. To discover the mindset and practices of abundance that lead to prosperity in our finances, our joy and our happiness, we often must unravel the parts of our money story that hold us back.

We have more dysfunctional views of money than politics and religion. A healthy view of money and a keen understanding of the money-making model of our business allows any of us career women as employees to be more valuable and relevant in our careers to fuel our growth and the growth of our company.

Prosperity refers to more than a bank account. Prosperity is creating the mindset for abundance. The origin of the word *abundance* is rooted in the Latin word for *overflowing*.[6] We want our story to be overflowing with abundance in health, wealth, and happiness.

Rhythm

Our human existence is flow, not force; it's connection, not control. It's completely unrealistic to think all of our days should be good days. We live in an ebb and flow of emotions: highs, lows, and everything in between. As we look to overflow with abundance, we find it in rhythm. *Rhythm* comes from the word *rhein*, "to flow."[7] If we desire to live in overflow, we learn what it means to live in flow.

We connect story and money into an intentional rhythm. All of nature is based on rhythms. Rhythm is the marker of music, stories and art, signs of a life enjoyed, experienced, and well-lived.

The key of rhythm, like the seasons, unlocks the door to a life of flourishing, a much more satisfying human life than simply being productive. The word *flourishing* has floral origins, when the stem of a flower reaches up to the sun and its roots down through the soil.[8] Things that bloom and flourish with overflow and abundance are planted in the right conditions. For us to thrive, our conditions are story, money, and rhythm.

PART I
Story

CHAPTER 3
Why a Story?

W e've been using stories in our lives for eons to make sense of the world around us, from myths handed down through generations and pictures on the walls of caves, to parables in the Bible, our family photo albums, and info on the company website. Stories are the way we communicate as humans in the world. Stories are how we connect. Our brains are hardwired for connection through our stories, always looking for how we matter to each other. We crave connection. It's as important to our lives as food, water, and security.

Our stories matter. Like an epic book or film, they are full of dreams, emotions, struggles, lessons, meaning, and purpose. Our stories are even more valuable than our classroom education, degrees, and certifications.

Our story doesn't wait for us to be enough, to earn enough, to acquire enough. Our story doesn't wait for us to finish the degree, find the husband, or start the job. Our story doesn't end after the divorce or when you leave a company.

Our stories are being written each day, chapter by chapter. The question is, who's holding the pen? Our story to this point may have been written from someone else's script, such as our parents, teachers, coworker, or boss. To begin writing your own story, there is some undoing, some re-scripting. This isn't starting over. We don't go back and erase the past; we use it to teach us and propel us forward.

Take the pen and write the next chapters of your story with intention by listening to your head and heart. It's time to look within, to reflect on who you are and what you want the next chapters of your story to be. You're the lead character in your story, no more standing back and playing the supporting role or the stagehand.

You know the phrase about loving something from the bottom of your heart. I want you to fall in love with your story by reaching down into the depths of your soul, the bottom of your heart where those tiny embers can be fanned into flames.

You may be thinking, "Rebecca, I'm too old to start over," or "I've invested too much time in my career to make any changes," or "I've screwed up so much I don't know if I'll ever recover." You're not starting over; you're starting with a wealth of knowledge and experience you've already acquired. None of the life you've lived to this point is wasted or wrong; it's all a part of your story.

In fact, your story increases your value. This is an inherent truth about story. My absolute favorite illustration of the value of story comes from writers Rob Walker and Joshua Glenn in their experiment *Significant Objects*. Walker and Glenn purchased thrift store items for no more than $1.25 each. Writers were assigned to write descriptions, crafting beautiful fictional stories about the items. Would a powerful story increase the value of an otherwise common or even useless item? Turns out, yes, a story increases the value. Items purchased brought in over $8,000, which was then donated to charity.

A white mug with a black smiley face, originally purchased for $2, coupled with a beautiful story written by Ben Greeman, author of several books and an editor at *The New Yorker*, brought in $32.08. That's a 1,604 percent increase. Story adds value to our lives—and even to smiley face coffee mugs.

My favorite of the significant objects is the Tiny Jar of Mayo. You know those tiny individual serving jars of condiments you get when you order room service? A tiny jar of mayonnaise, acquired for free, sold for $51! Obviously they weren't buying the mayo, they were buying the story. The item's story, written by author Rick Moody, is full of passion and expletives.[9] I've read it several times, and it still doesn't completely make sense to me, but every time I read it, I get a little something different from it—and isn't that the marker of a great story? Isn't that the way we're supposed to live our lives, as one big story, written chapter by chapter, and as we read back over those chapters, we get a little something new from it we can use to take us into the next?

All of our experiences, hopes, and dreams are stored in our brain as stories.

The Story Center

Picture your brain as a giant story center. This is the library of you. With all the experiences and information we've gathered in our lives, our brains are a busy place. There are stories we hear, stories we tell ourselves, stories we dream and imagine. There's the wall with all the books you've ever read, the viewing room of all the movies, TED Talks, and videos you've watched. There's the community room with all your past relationships and random chance encounters, the bosses, the neighbors, the family, the loves you've lived, and those you've lost.

The senses room holds the heat and smell of blazing summer sun melting hot asphalt underfoot as you walk the country road to Grandma's, oozing with independence and the perfume that brings back all the anticipation of new love. The smell of the art room at school calling you to create, the glide of a new pen across a new journal page, signifying new beginnings. The warm smell of a child's hair after a sweaty day of playing outside. There's the nerves and sweaty armpits from your first job, the victory of your first promotion, the thrill from the meeting where you spoke up and they loved your idea.

The imagination room overflows with the stories you make up. This room has a full range of darkness and light. It includes your dreams for the future, and the worries of catastrophes you dream up while lying in bed waiting for your teen with a new driver's license to come home. The story center is full of happy stories, angry stories, scary stories, hurt- and pain-filled stories. We're using our stories to make choices every day. Our lives are a constant of emotions. The more emotion attached to the story, the more likely we will recall the information when we need it and often when we don't. Emotions strengthen memory.

We are continually taking in information and organizing it into the story room. Picture a crazy librarian running around trying to put all of our stories away and figuring out how to catalog them. In fact, our brains catalog and consolidate our stories as we sleep. This is a significant reason to get plenty of sleep so the librarian can do her job. How many times have you said to someone you love, "If you'd just put it away, you could find it when you need it." The same goes for you and your sleep. When you sleep, the information from the day gets filed away to find it when you need it.

As a high achiever, sometimes the story room is stimulating and exciting. Some days the story room won't let us sleep, either with the bright light of our dreams shining in our eyes or the shadowy dark corners of our mistakes haunting us through the night.

Some stories won't go away even if we want them to. In my story room is the embarrassing time I brought cola products to a meeting I was hosting at a plant that is run by an opposing cola company. The plant manager asked who had brought in the drinks lined up on the table, the table full of their competitor's cola products in large two- liter bottles, their labels billboards of insult. I slowly raised my hand while turning ghostly pale, wishing to magically disappear. This story reminds me always to know who's in the room, which has benefited me in thousands of interactions since. All of your experiences go into the story room: the child of you, the awkward growing up of you, all of your business decisions, successes, failures, interactions with your colleagues—all of it.

Let this image of your story center inform you of the complete ridiculousness and impossibility of separating our personal lives and work lives. We have one life, full of all of our experiences and stories. It's the collective of these stories we call upon daily. Sometimes these stories inspire us forward into something greater, and sometimes they hinder or halt us, keeping us striving or stuck.

I'll be going about a regular day and think of a random story from twenty years ago. Sometimes the memory is an inspired one, like the time I had the opportunity to work directly with Dr. Stephen R. Covey, one of the most outstanding thought leaders of our time. There's a particular exchange with a prominent place in my story center. After traveling together for three days speaking in three cities, Dr. Covey looked at me and said, "You're a teacher." Today, more than two decades later, his comment continues to give me confidence and affirms my desire to help and serve.

Some voices create troublesome memories that threaten to hold us back. Nearly everyone I know has a story from a coach, teacher, or parent that haunts them today, giving them pause about their truth, their worth, and their potential. I use these troubling memories as a reminder of the immense responsibility I have in choosing the words I share with others, knowing how our stories connect and influence each other. Genuine and affirming words are a powerful force in the world. Own this role as the writer of your story. Take full use of the power you possess inside you right now to write the next chapters of an epic story.

As an executive coach, I have the privilege of meandering through the story centers of beautifully powerful humans doing important work. I recently worked with a marketing executive at a rapidly growing tech start-up. She struggled to see herself as the leader she needed to be, facing growing responsibility and demands. Without an executive title on her résumé prior to this role, her days were ruled by feelings of inadequacy and impostor syndrome. I was able to pull the story out of her archives from the days she played collegiate soccer. As an athlete, most of her days were leading winning teams. As she discussed a challenge with the business and her employees, I asked how she would have handled this on the soccer field. A smile of confidence washed over her face immediately as she realized she had the skills for the challenge and this role. She'd been leading and building teams on the soccer fields for more years than she'd been in business. Newly equipped with her own story, she walked into the next board meeting as the leader she truly was.

This story center is our soul. It is the collective of our humanity, personal, emotional, and social. We're feeding our souls through stories and experiences throughout our lives, and all of it matters.

Will you do something with me for a few minutes? I'd love you to go on a quick tour of your story center. Take three big deep breaths, all the way in and all the way out. Let your shoulders, your face, and your jaw relax. Now close your eyes and wander around in your stories for a few minutes to reflect on the awe of you, which is the all of you. Feel those stories. I'll be here to continue as your Thrive Guide when you get back.

Life Is Long

How did it go? My hope is that you're seeing how much love, life, and experience you already possess. I hope you're feeling this sense that life is long and you've got so much more to explore. Yes, this contradicts the "life is short" messages we tend to throw on our social media pages. "Life is short" is from a quote in a William Shakespeare play,[10] which would have had much more validity in 1500s England when life expectancy was thirty-nine years.[11] Sure, some circumstances end beautiful lives early. But the "life is short" message puts us in striving mode with the hurry to "have it all and do it all *now*" approach. *Hurry and figure it out, rush, get rich quick, hack, better, faster, more, command and control!* This gives me shivers of anxiety just thinking about it. We dive into the world expecting quick success and putting pressure on ourselves to do it.

A life lived curiously, noticing what we love and why we love it—that's how a story unfolds. It's the intentional act of being curious of our thoughts and emotions that takes us on a journey to discover our depths, our soul, and our essence. This journey takes time. Life is a marathon, not a sprint. The hustle and hurry culture needs to end. Let's get excited to wonder, wander, and to explore our interests and ideas. When you begin to see your story for the whole life journey that it is, life is long. A woman's average life expectancy in the United States is around eighty years.[12] That's plenty of time to explore.

This hurry up and get caught up isn't helping us to explore and appreciate our story. All the years matter. We're not wasting time; we're exploring. We're only wasting time when we stop listening to our soul and stop respecting our thoughts, ideas, emotions, and struggles. As we reflect on our lives, we learn more about ourselves; this informs us and leads us forward to explore more, evolve, change, and grow.

Ready to write a story of growth? Ready to take the pen even if your hand shakes? It's okay because we're all a little afraid.

CHAPTER 4
We're All a Little Afraid

s we evolve, we face resistance. We feel the pull of old scripts and patterns asking us to stay: stay stuck, stay struggling, stay safe. This is where I remind you that you're not a machine here to produce; you are a beautiful human, and writing your own story makes you an artist and a creator. Ask anyone who creates, and they will tell you there are two aspects of creating:

1. They can't "not" do it—it comes from deep in their soul.
2. Sharing your creations with the imperfect world takes vulnerability, grit, and guts.

Some of the greatest creators don't make it past number two. There are life-changing inventions, solutions, and works of art buried in someone's head, their heart, their hard drive, or their basement because they didn't make it past the fear and uncertainty to bring it into the world. When the story of your life and career come from your soul, it is so personal and emotional. And because we are social beings, we desperately want people to like it. This is the challenge that often separates those willing to write their own story from those who are seeking permission, copying someone else's story, or letting someone else write it for them.

Because we're human, with the human ability to think and overthink, every one of us has fears and insecurities.

> Everything you've ever wanted is on the other side of fear.
>
> —George Addair[13]

Crossing the Sea of Uncertainty

Everything we want isn't actually on the other side of fear; it's on the other side of the Sea of Uncertainty.

Dr. Joan Rosenberg, author of *90 Seconds to a Life You Love*, teaches us on a podcast episode that *fear* is only the appropriate word if there is physical or imminent danger. If a tiger walks into your office, you should be afraid. If there's a tornado coming at your house, you should be afraid. Otherwise, what you're dealing with is *uncertainty*. Uncertainty is that blank space between what you know and what you don't know. Fear requires immediate action. Get out of the room where the tiger is, get in the basement during the tornado—this is our fight-or-flight response. However, uncertainty doesn't often need immediate action. Because of our bias to control, uncertainty is seen as a problem to fix. What we first need is some perspective to help us determine "the rest of the story and then decide if we need a response."[14]

Picture yourself looking out over a vast sea. On the other side is something you want, the career you want, the changes you want to make, the chances you want to take. You can choose to see this sea of uncertainty as churning waves with whitecaps too dangerous to cross. Or you can choose to acknowledge the sea and get to work assuring yourself you can craft the right plan to swim, build a boat, or backstroke across to get to what you want on the other side of the Sea of Uncertainty.

But we rarely have all the information in the story, especially in business. We aren't sure if the marketing plan is going to bring us the right customers. We don't know if Jane in accounting is going to get her act together or if we need to fire her. We don't know if we're getting the promotion. Every single day we live with uncertainty waiting for us to cross over it to get what we want, be where we want to be, achieve what we want to achieve.

First Responders

The first voice speaking to our fear and insecurity is our own. We are the first responders on the edge of the Sea of Uncertainty. The role of a first responder is to stop the emergency from progressing. How you speak to yourself is critical. A first responder will diagnose the situation. If you were in a car accident, a first responder isn't going to start berating you for your driving skills. Can you imagine a firefighter rolling up to your accident scene screaming, "What are you, an idiot? How fast were you going? Do you know how to drive?" A real response would likely be, "Are you okay? I'm here to help you." Take on the role of a first responder in your story; speak with love, care, and concern and the desire to help and move yourself forward.

As we talk to ourselves as first responders, we have several "inside voices" available to us. It's up to us to choose to listen and to choose the right combination of voices for the situation. When we personify our inside voices, we can treat them as key relationships and characters in our thrive story. These are lifetime characters in our story. We write them in and out of various chapters as we need them, but they're always with us.

All the voices in our head:
- Little Bitch: Our inner critic
- Judge Jury: Whose fault is it?
- Curious Toddler: Why?
- Scientist: Fact finder
- Dreamer: Visionary
- Thrive Guide: Our deep inner knowing

The first voice that typically shows up is the Little Bitch. She's the inner critic; her specialty is impostor syndrome. She keeps an external hard drive full of your past mistakes from your story center and is ready to plug it in at any moment. *Remember that time you ... (insert embarrassing thing you've been trying to forget for ten years). You're not going to do that are you? That seems really dumb. She looked at you funny in the meeting; she probably doesn't like you.* The Little Bitch in your head is relentless, and she's a lifer. We can't kill her out of our story. We can't out-career her or pay her off with a high enough salary. She's forever. So, we put her in the passenger seat with a seat belt and a snack, but she doesn't get to drive. We acknowledge her because she's real; we just don't respond to her ramblings.

Judge Jury is ready to point her finger at someone to blame. Some cultures call her Karen. Judge Jury wants to see the manager. She wants to call a lawyer. There's got to be someone responsible for this!

Look, here's the deal. You will be wronged many, many times in this lifetime. The bolder you are, the more people will come at you. Recognize the voice and then ask yourself, *Will spending energy to find who's at fault serve me well in calming the Sea of Uncertainty, or will it only create more waves?*

The Curious Toddler constantly wants to know why and what's next, insatiable in her curiosity. If you've raised children, you remember the toddler stage: When they begin to talk and ask WHY about EVERYTHING until you, as the responsible parent, begin hiding in the bathroom faking intestinal issues just to have a few minutes away from all the freaking questions. They gather outside, sticking their fingers under the door, still asking, "Why mommy, why? Can you see my fingers under the door? How many fingers? How long are you going to be?"

Being curious is a natural part of the human experience and important when navigating the Sea of Uncertainty. It's no accident toddlers immediately begin asking *why* when they discover language.

It's a deep part of our humanity. And one we can use more deliberately in our life and career.

The more successful we become in our career and the more we actually DO know, we begin to dial down the curiosity, sometimes replacing it with assumptions. Or our ego becomes rattled when we DON'T know the answer, so we push on, hoping no one will know that we DON'T know. To navigate the Sea of Uncertainty, reclaim your Curious Toddler voice—stick your fingers under the door more often to ask why. Curiosity transmits dopamine to our brain's reward circuit, and studies show it enhances memory and learning. Ask why and then follow that curiosity around for a bit.

The Scientist voice wants cause and effect, data, and more information. Sometimes this is helpful for clarity and context, but sometimes you just can't gather data on a feeling or an instinct.

I created a seven-month Rise & Thrive Experience for career women designed to transform their lives. I had no data or facts to comfort me that it was going to work. It was an innovative idea, and I was launching into unknown territory. Now, if you're installing a new bathtub, you should measure and get the data, but when we're following our instincts and our dreams, we don't always have data to back it up. This can be rough because in business we've had it drilled into our heads that we want a solid return on investment and to do our due diligence. I get it, but sometimes it's either not what you need, or it doesn't exist. I wonder how many groundbreaking innovations have been stopped short because there wasn't enough data to back it up. Real innovation comes from swimming forward in the Sea of Uncertainty without the data, without the external validation that it will work, when your Thrive Guide is leading from your inner knowing.

While the Curious Toddler wants to know why, the Dreamer wants to know why not? We all have a Dreamer, the voice that comes from that place at the bottom of our hearts where the love lives. Picture a room full of toddlers: some are climbing the walls, some are playing together, some are quietly coloring, and some are in the corner sulking and sad. This pretty much describes the various personality types of our Dreamers. Some are bold and leading our choices, and some are sulking and sad.

We need our dreams, which means we need to take a look at the personality of our Dreamer. Does she need a friend to lure her out of the corner? Does she need a coach to help her trust herself again? Does she need an implementation specialist to help these dreams become reality? Our Dreamer often needs someone to hold the microphone and let her speak. We need our Dreamer to help us in Crossing the Sea of Uncertainty. She needs reflection and connection. Making changes in our life requires us to envision what we want. What will it feel like when we get there? Nurture your Dreamer; she's a peach.

And finally, the most helpful and kind of all our inner voices, the Thrive Guide. She's done her homework, like a Sherpa preparing for our mountain climb. Your Inner Thrive Guide knows your hopes, dreams, and your talents. She knows your insecurities and your soft spots. She is the librarian of your story center. She knows just the information you need when you need it. She wants what is best for you. In fact, she's the voice of God that speaks your language, knows your heart and your desires, and will help you plot your course if you let her. She's the voice of your intuition that also reaches out to hear the other inner voices and distills them into the next best step for you to take.

All of these voices are inside of you and all make appearances. Our role is to discern which voice is showing up and whom we really need to hear from. Developing the voice of our Thrive Guide ensures crossing the Sea of Uncertainty will be relatively safe and maybe even scenic. During this book, I'm your Thrive Guide, helping you to recognize your own voice and make it clear and concise. Then you'll take over the role to continue writing your story.

Take some comfort in knowing the fear and insecurity you feel is a natural part of our human experience. To do the big, bold, beautiful work we want to do, to have a life we choose, we need some perspective and strategies to deal with uncertainty. It's not going away; we don't outgrow it, out-career it, or pay it off with a bigger bonus. We learn to live with it with a few strategies:

- Use the word *uncertainty* instead of *fear* to not put yourself into fight or flight mode and see the waters as restless and dangerous.
- We can use taking a break in stillness to see the waters as calm. Picture yourself floating across the sea or calmly using strokes of swimming rather than expending all your energy flailing and striving.
- Use words rooted in faith, belief, intuition, and past experiences to lead you confidently while crafting a plan that rises up from the Inner Thrive Guide.
- Continually crossing the Sea of Uncertainty builds confidence.

The Sea of Uncertainty will always exist. We're never done doing the work of growth. Those you look up to have all crossed that great and sometimes turbulent sea to bring what you so respect into the world. I know sometimes it can feel like you're the only one.

Because uncertainty is a part of our human experience, it can be a means of connecting. Twelve years into a wildly successful sales and consulting career, I was asked to speak to our western region and share a little about my success. Ugh. While this should have felt like an honor and a privilege, what it did was douse gasoline on my insecurity fire.

I came prepared to talk about using our customer relationship management (CRM) tool effectively, prospecting, and building a business case—all of the company-approved messages that would help the district manager reinforce the overall theme of business: control, measure, optimize. These are important. I do believe in the power of great systems and controls for our businesses. I also know that my success in sales is based largely on my ability to use my gut intuition and to ask great questions to connect with my clients in a beautiful, human way. This is harder to teach. So I stuck with the control, measure, optimize topics that seem easier to replicate across the business.

The presentation went well. I was minutes from changing into my comfy clothes and getting ready to belly up to the hotel bar with some of my favorite people whom I got to see only once or twice a year in person. (These human-to-human sessions are the ones that build our joy and love of the job. They're rare and special.) I asked the obligatory, "What questions do you have?" I don't remember exactly how it was phrased, but someone asked something like, "How do you hit your numbers year over year?" It's a fair question for a salesperson, because successful salespeople are rewarded with higher goals each year. Sometimes you actually fear hitting the goal in anticipation of how hard it will be to hit the *next* year's goal.

My answer was honest and simple, I think partly because I was hoping it would get me out of there quicker. "Well, I'm afraid every single day."

This wasn't in my notes; it wasn't on my mind prior to that moment, it was an authentic human response to a human question. It was in that moment the entire vibe of the room shifted. Those who had been politely pretending to listen all of a sudden sat up and took real notice. The young woman who asked the question looked relieved. The emotion in the room changed so much I flashed a look to the manager to see if somehow my response was going to be her demise. She didn't look angry or terrified, so I continued to answer the follow-up questions that were now coming quickly. At least five hands raised immediately.

The first follow-up question. "You? You're afraid?" I took that one as a compliment because I had a bold reputation in the way I approached my business and the solutions I'd built for my clients, not always complying with the standard operating procedures.

"Yes, every damn day, I'm a little afraid," I said. "Afraid I won't hit the month or the quarter or the year. Afraid this is the year the company figures out I have no idea what I'm doing and they find out I'm a fraud—a top-performing fraud skimming by year over year with some miraculous deal that didn't actually come through the way we teach that it will; therefore, I can't replicate it, so every month, every year, I'm kind of winging it."

The entire room was enthralled, leaning forward, some taking notes. This memory of mine is more vivid years after the actual experience because of how the next few years played out in my career at this company. This was the meeting where my personal brand increased in the company. The human connections I made in that room that day still live on. The relationships with that team and the ripple effect of that ten minutes from my hour time slot still live on today. I promise you nobody remembers a damn thing I said about how important it is to use the CRM, but everyone remembers the collective sigh of relief and then the wave of confidence that shot through the room after a top-ten company performer admitted her fear.

"If you're not a little afraid every day, you're probably not doing it right," I added. "I can't imagine what this job would be like without that tug of fear pushing me past my comfort zone constantly. I honestly believe if I get too comfortable, it's probably time to quit." That was an act of prophecy because that's exactly what happened five years later.

The conversations continued in the bar that night. People came by my table and asked more questions, asked to schedule some time with me after the conference. Seasoned veterans and newbies alike relished in my speaking in my out-loud voice the things they carried deep in their hearts.

I'm confident I set a lot of us free that day, myself included. I set us free from the shame and hiding we thought was necessary when we believed we were the only ones carrying the burden of fear and insecurities. Our human stories connected in a beautiful, human way. With that freedom to be human, then we could get back to work, use the CRM, practice the value proposition, ask for the business. Now the conversation was out of our heads and sitting at the bar with us beside a cosmo and a cabernet. I knew the topic had resonated because even the teetotalers came into the bar to get a piece of this human experience. Like art, music, and pets, the shared human experience of fear and insecurity gathers us into community and social well-being.

CHAPTER 5

Your Uniqueness Is
Your Superpower

N ow that we're on this journey through uncertainty together, it's time to explore our uniqueness as our superpower. We are each equipped with unique talents. Your uniqueness is exactly what God intended. And great news, you already have it. You already have within you everything you need to thrive. The answer isn't "out there"; it's within us.

Hold on. Don't gloss over this like it's just a lunchbox note from your mom. Look at your hands, turn them over, and look at your fingerprints. We are each unique in every way, down to our fingerprints. God was not into the die-cast manufacturing of humans.

This is so fundamental and yet, do we honor our uniqueness? Do we truly know our uniqueness in a way we can use it as an advantage? Do we seek it out as our superpower? Do we honor and look for the uniqueness in others? Or do we strive and compare? Do we slide to the back, hoping not to be fully seen?

Don't worry. We're not writing our story for perfection; we're writing our story for connection.

Let's use childhood games to illustrate the point. Picture yourself holding a handful of marbles. They're all beautiful, round, and shiny. You stare at your hand, mesmerized by their perfection and beauty. Now, turn your hand over. Place the marbles in the center of the table in front of you. They all roll away. Marbles as beautiful and perfect as they are on their own don't stick together. Perfection blocks connection.

Now picture a handful of jigsaw puzzle pieces, each piece with its jaggedy-ass edges and dust from the bottom of the box. You place the puzzle pieces in the middle of the table. Then, with intention, you turn each piece over, looking for the beautiful side, the one with the picture that tells a story. Each piece is a tiny part of a bigger picture, looking to be a part of it. Some are edges, meant to hold it all together. Some are colorful and immediately stand out. Some are intricate and frustrating. Some are prominent and immediately find their matches.

As you begin to arrange the puzzle pieces, you're searching for how they connect. It takes focus and intention, but slowly you see the picture unveiling itself. The more you see the picture unfold before your eyes, the more excited you are to continue looking for another piece and another piece. And then you see it, the big picture, the story clicked together, each piece with its ins and outs, every piece different, yet they fit together. *Click. Click. Click.* It takes all of the pieces to create the picture—each one critical to the story and the structure. There are three important characteristics to a puzzle once it's put together: it's far more beautiful, it's stronger, and each piece matters.

On the other hand, marbles are created for a game meant for competition. Bigger marbles knock other marbles out of the game. Haven't we spent far too long working to be shiny, round, perfect marbles here to compete for bigger and better, battling to knock the others out of the game for the top spot? Isn't it time to see life and business as a means to connect, grow healthier, stronger, and more beautiful together? Isn't it time to see our uniqueness, differences, and jaggedy-ass edges as our strength and our own part of the bigger picture?

Consider when you lost your appreciation for your uniqueness. Mine started in school. In school, our individuality starts to be a liability, not an asset. In those first few years of life, our family members clapped with every funny face or our first steps. All those years Mom and Dad raised us up, praised us for just being us. Then school wanted us to sit down, be quiet, and be like everyone else. Someone rated and ranked us with grades and decided whether we moved to the next class. Envision this: you're a beautiful child, and at age five or six you move into a system where raising your hand is required to have an opinion. Oftentimes your hand-raising is not met with love and adoration; it's seen as a disruption. *Sit still … Do what you're told … No, it's not time to go to the bathroom … Color inside the lines … Follow directions … Be a good boy or girl. Good* means organized, on time, and smart. Everything else is unacceptable. We traded beautifully unique for controlled and compliant because it was easier on the system—a system designed to control, measure, and optimize.

In school we began to ask, "Am I normal? Am I good? Am I bad?" Being "normal" means we're "good." Being organized and compliant means we're better. The word *normal* comes from the Latin word *norma*, which means[15] "carpenter's square." *Normal* isn't a word that works to describe people; it's to measure things and make them consistently the same. As I like to remind people, *normal* is just a setting on the dryer.

The same goes for words like *good, bad, right, wrong,* or *perfect* when we're describing people, including ourselves. We use these words to help us deal with the uncertainty that comes from the infinite number of ways we are actually different. We're not wrong; we're just different.

Please note: I'm not down on teachers. I love the humans who choose teaching as a profession. I know many teachers want to love and teach their students as beautiful individuals. I want to be really clear about how much I love humans who go out of their way to pour wisdom into our youth. I'm down on a system that values standardization and efficiency over humanity and uniqueness.

I love the way Carol Sanford describes our uniqueness in episode fifty-three of my podcast, *The Badass Women's Council*. Carol teaches about essence. Not just our unique skills and background, but also the pure essence of our uniqueness akin to our fingerprints.[16]

When working with my coaching clients, I ask them to list their talents. Instead of using an assessment, I want them to reflect on these and get comfortable knowing themselves, listening to their Inner Thrive Guide. It's always an interesting exercise. The first response is usually a long, quiet stare with a slow *blink ... blink*. Then a stumbling response like, "I'm not sure I have any." These are typically high achievers, CEOs, and vice presidents who have done amazing work—seasoned veterans in their careers. It's fascinating. Then I say, "Yes you do. Everyone does ... no wrong answers, just throw something out there." They start to throw out some roles they play. "I'm a good mom," or "I'm a good leader." I remind them that's a role and that the deeper question is, "What makes you uniquely great at those roles?" This is difficult for everyone at first.

With the number of personality profile tools available in the world today and how widely used they are in business, it seems we'd all have a firm grasp of our "self." Yet we don't. In fact, many of the personality assessments are used for more comparison, much like our grades in school. These assessments go only so far.

These tests categorize us into groups; they don't really get to our individual essence. There's a tendency then to use our category as our definition of self. I've seen a personality profile become a banner to hold up to defend independence versus to create connection. So at its worst it does more to divide us than connect us. These assessments also further our reliance on external validation rather than deeply knowing ourselves and being curious about others. To be fair, I've taken every assessment available! I don't believe there was malicious intent on designing them. In some cases, I've seen them help leaders to understand that not everyone on their team sees the world as they see the world. It can be a great starting point; however, we need to dig deeper and continue to reflect throughout our lives on who we are.

Once my clients start making their list of what makes them unique individuals, the conversation starts to run more freely. My favorite question is what their fourteen-year-old self was doing for fun. Our uniqueness unfolds over our lifetime of experiences, *and* we were created as unique from the beginning. If we can tap into that young person's sense of self just as they were expressing their independence before the world started to set expectations, we can catch a glimpse of our essence and then look for the thread that weaves together our life's experiences.

How would the world change if we stood tall in our uniqueness as our superpower? How would our confidence change? How would we show up to meetings differently? How would the world change if, instead of looking to compare and compete, we sought out the uniqueness in others?

What if we moved through life infinitely and courageously curious about people and their stories? What if we actually looked at the ways we are different as clues to find the pieces of our puzzle? Think of someone right now who drives you a little crazy. Their differences feel frustrating. Now ask yourself, what value do they add to your life, your work, your story? We need different; we need our uniqueness and the uniqueness of others.

Using Your Gut: There's No Class on Intuition

There's no class on intuition because it is a part of ourselves. Our Inner Thrive Guide organizes our collection of stories and experiences for us to call upon, often without conscious awareness. We just know. We use our gut in life and business. It's as much a part of our career skill set as communication and leadership. The very best leaders have an intuitive sense about people and their needs and motivations. They ask good questions, then lean in to hear people's hearts. They create teams built on trust and human connection. They've learned to trust their

Inner Thrive Guide as a part of their talents. I shudder to think how many great leaders were passed over for a promotion because great gut instinct and intuition aren't widely respected on a résumé.

I was blessed to work for an amazing business owner, Don Taylor. Don started a company that specialized in staffing for light industrial manufacturing in small-town markets in the Midwest. He hired mostly energetic young women with skills in customer service as account representatives. I was in my mid-twenties, and my work experiences prior to this were wiping sweat from tanning beds, selling office supplies, and serving food and drinks (but not at the same time).

Don was highly involved in teaching young recruits like me the basics of the business. He trained us to interview and place people in jobs and gave us an unforgettable Business Management 101 degree in the process. Don was unashamed about "gut feeling" being a perfectly acceptable reason to make business decisions. In fact, it was his instruction.

We learned how to ask great questions to help place the right person in the right job. We kept track of *turnover*, or in other words, the number of placements we made each week and the number of times we had to replace someone because they weren't a good fit. Low turnover was a measure of our success in the role. The people I placed typically stayed and succeeded in their roles, but I will never forget one of our meetings discussing turnover.

Don and I looked at my placement numbers and the few times I had turnover with clients. He asked me a very simple but profound question, "Did you go against your gut?" Without hesitation I could look at the examples of when the candidate hadn't worked out, and each time I had a "feeling" it wasn't a great placement. Either pressured by client deadlines or my own ego wanting to meet weekly measures, I had gone against my gut and made a placement anyway. Each time those proved to be expensive decisions that had a short-term gain and a longer-term expensive loss in replacing the person. Had I left the role open a few days longer to find the right placement, it would have been far more valuable for our business, the client, and both of the candidates.

Here I was with no college degree at the time, a healthy appetite for beer, pizza, and a rockin' Saturday night, and the CEO of a company was telling me to trust my gut to make decisions for his business. This remains one of the greatest gifts I've ever been given. I paid attention to my gut like I paid attention to the forms we filled out for each placement. Gut feeling is a powerful force in our life and business. Each time my gut served me with a great placement or saved me from making a terrible one, my confidence in this precious thing called intuition grew.

If deadlines were looming and the candidates weren't matching, I became confident saying to my clients, "I just don't feel good about the people I have right now, and I'd rather wait until we get a better fit for your company." Their trust in me grew, knowing I was looking out for them. I was so confident in this use of my intuition, I would have gladly put on my résumé under skills, "Uses Microsoft Word and has a mad use of her gut instincts."

Fast forward to working for an international training and consulting company as a sales professional. I had just gained a new boss. There was territory realignment and the shuffling of the deck that comes with change. In those changes, I was acquiring a few new clients. One of the clients just didn't sit well with me. There was this "feeling" I was not the right person to manage this account.

I had grown so comfortable over the years using my intuition to make decisions, and this one wasn't sitting well. It was sending my Sea of Uncertainty into turbulent waves. To this day I can remember the stretch of highway I was driving as I talked to my new boss from my car about the new territory alignment. We got to the client in question, I paused slightly, and I said, "I can't tell you why. It's just a feeling in my gut, but I don't think I'm the right person to manage that account."

"That's not how we make business decisions," he responded. "If you can't provide a more specific reason, we're going forward with the account lists, and you'll be fine."

That's paraphrased a bit since this was more than ten years ago, but I remember the general vibe of the conversation and the wake-up call that not all leaders were Don Taylor, and maybe I wasn't as smart as I thought I was. Maybe using my gut was just a tactic for young career people in small towns and as you got older you were supposed to have more PowerPoint presentations and degrees and charts to validate your thoughts and decisions. Maybe going with your gut was for rookies, and facts were for professionals.

Fortunately for me, my lessons learned from Don Taylor had run deeply enough in my story center that I was able to continue to call upon my intuition and to trust it. But I spent many years overcomplicating things, looking for more data and information to validate my gut feelings. I wondered if this new boss was smarter, since this was a bigger company. My job had actually had an MBA requirement, but they overlooked that requirement for me. This message ran in the background of my story center for many years: *You weren't really qualified. You're the outsider without the MBA, and this will eventually be your undoing. Smart people don't "go with their gut."*

The more I sold and the more successful I became in this company, I realized it was largely based on listening to my intuition. I became a master at asking great questions from my gut instinct. I was able to rekindle my confidence in my intuition. Intuition isn't some magical fairy dust; it's the accumulation of your experiences logged into your story center. There's no test every day of what I know; there's the confidence that I know many things from years of experience, and those memories are logged in my story center. I trust myself to recall things as I need them. And God does a great job of providing the librarian in my brain to give me what I need when I need it, as long as I get enough sleep.

This new boss would later become a great friend and is a tremendous supporter still today. He later wrote a best-selling book, *Management Mess to Leadership Success*, so he has come clean that he made a few mistakes. He was learning too. We're all humans, learning, making mistakes, and adjusting to do better. Puzzles, not marbles.

I taught my kids at a very young age about their intuition. "You know that funny feeling in your belly when something doesn't seem right? That's God speaking to you. Listen. Always trust your tummy." Those early sleepover days, letting my kids be away overnight, were strange and uncertain for all of us. As they'd leave, I'd remind them, "If you're around people that make your tummy feel funny, call me and say, 'My tummy feels funny. I want to come home.' I'll come and get you; no one will ask any questions. It doesn't have to mean you're going to throw up sick; it can mean you know you shouldn't be there and you want to come home." This is a good lesson in every chapter of your story, from seven to ninety-seven.

As I listen to people question their intuition when it doesn't measure up with a college syllabus or a comment from a manager, I cringe. I pray we learn to trust ourselves, our Inner Thrive Guides, and not need constant validation from others. It's too easy to have our story written by someone else.

Honor the wealth of experience and emotions you have inside your story center. We make decisions on emotions within our subconscious and then try to validate those decisions with facts and data. It is our emotional flow that is constantly informing our decisions about life, work, people, strategies, and even what to have for dinner. By trying to control our life and dismiss the emotional flow into one of more control and consistency, we block the very emotional nature of our lives and our decisions. We prevent our inner-knowing Thrive Guide from speaking the truth.

A client recently told me of a product development concern she had with her new company, one that could negatively affect its clients. She's new to executive leadership and still building her confidence. She had shared this with the leadership team, but they seemed unconcerned.

Because she was new and still a little uncertain, she didn't persist. But she couldn't shake the feeling that there was a problem. I explained that she was hired for her role to bring her gut feelings that come from her experience. I encouraged her to go back to the team, to again share her concern but this time with the clarity and context of her experiences, what had happened in the company she had worked for previously, and how it was triggering a gut response for her now.

We are built to feel, process, and use our emotions of love, joy, disappointment, anger, and every other emotion you can think of. Why wouldn't we use them in our work? I looked and I simply can't find an off button for our emotions, not a literal one at least. But we sure use lots of things to dull them when we don't want to feel them: booze, food, shopping; the list of numbing tactics is long. We even hold back on the joyful, loving emotions at work with phrases like "Don't get your hopes up" and "Don't get too attached."

Getting your hopes up is raising your level of belief, and it is precisely the thing that we need to elevate our careers and grow. Get attached to something that matters deeply to you and see how that changes your commitment.

Fall in Love with Your Story

I have a few simple questions to help get you thinking about who you are. Let yourself gain a deeper appreciation for the chapters of your story you've already lived. These past experiences, the successes and the struggles, are all a part of your story, and they're clues to your essence. We'll use the acronym LOVE to use loving and kind eyes as you explore your story.

L: What have you learned?

The classes you've taken, the books you've read, the academic type of learning—what are those things that stand out from your academic life? Not everything from your academic learning is relevant to your present and your future. Some things you simply endured while you learned to be compliant to the education system. And there are things you've learned that spoke to your heart and led you wanting to know more. Take some time in reflection on what you've learned so far in your story and what you want to carry forward or revisit. Go back to middle school, high school, college; what were the things that really captured your heart and your mind? Then go deeper. What was it about those classes that spoke to you?

O: What have you overcome?
Life is messy, with challenges and tragedy, some leading to trauma. In each of these we learn about ourselves. We learn about how we interact with other humans. It's not the challenge itself; it's the rising up and the overcoming where we learn more about ourselves. Sometimes our mess can become a key part of our message in future chapters of our story. What are those lessons and beautiful bits that you want to gather from the rubble of your struggles and carry with you as a beautiful reminder of your resilience and a soft spot you'll use to connect with empathy and vulnerability to serve another?

V: What have you verified?
To verify is to establish the truth, accuracy, or reality of something, what is true and accurate for YOU. What is true for one of us may not be true for another. There are few universal truths and far more personal truths. Universal truths are things like gravity and entropy. We each have personal truths for ourselves that we've verified through experience. From simple things like this: I feel my most confident when my hair is shoulder length. I've tried to be a short-haired girl, and nope, that's not for me. I've tested this theory enough times to know it's true. Now it's a part of my personal truth. No matter how many pictures of cute short haircuts I see, I know not to try that again!

I also know I am a builder and creator. I don't do well following someone else's script. I have verified this through my work enough times to know it would be silly for me to try and do anything but build my own business or to work in a career that gives me the freedom to build and create. This may not be true for you. It shouldn't be true for everyone.

I have verified through tests and trials that my best writing happens early in the morning. My schedule should reflect this verified truth by leaving space for writing early in the day and not booking other appointments thinking I'll get writing done at night. Other writers have different truths.

I know I'm more patient and kinder before 9 p.m., so I taught my kids if they wanted to have tough conversations or talk through things they cared about, it would be way better to do that before 9 p.m.

What are your verified truths, things you've learned through personal experience? By reflecting on what we've verified, we learn to trust ourselves and become confident in our choices. This is one where people struggle a bit. I recommend you make this a weekly reflection practice. Each week, glance back over the week and ask yourself what you verified as a personal truth. You can then look for patterns that emerge.

E: What lights up your emotions?

Emotions are an integral part of our decision-making process, but they aren't always valued when making business decisions. We have a tendency to put far more weight on data and spreadsheets. Yet great marketers know we make decisions based on emotion and validate those decisions with facts. When writing our personal thrive story, emotions get a leading role because behavior and emotions come from the limbic system located deep within the brain. It is in the limbic system where we learn to manage the responses to emotions, retrieve memories from the story center, and understand the bigger picture. The limbic system houses mood, motivation, and judgment, a trifecta for writing a human story that is personal, emotional, and social.

When I ask you to consider what lights up your emotions, this could be a wide range. All strong emotions are clues to the things we care deeply about. To be motivated each day, those things that heighten emotions are clues to your personal story. In my thrive story, I get sad and angry when I see people in isolation, especially when that isolation comes from being different. This comes from my son's experiences with ADHD and watching him struggle to find a place of belonging in his early years.

When I see my clients begin to light up about an idea or a newfound awareness of their gifts and talents and how they are relevant to their career, I jump up and down and dance around my office clapping. True story. I tear up when someone tells me a connection I've made for them is helping them or their business. Emotions are clues to your personal story meant to guide you into the next chapters. Note those things that spark emotions in you. Once you jot them down, you'll be more aware as they surface. These also are clues to your essence.

Once you've jotted down your responses to these questions, read back through what you've written. Underline or highlight things that really stand out. What are the themes you see rising? These are clues of your inner knowing and your thrive story. This isn't a strategic planning session; this is you becoming more familiar with you, looking for those ideas, thoughts, and feelings you take into your next chapters. As I explored my story, the theme of connection was prevalent. I know this is a significant part of my purpose because it shows up in all aspects of my story.

Now let's ask some more specific questions.

- What are your unique talents?
- What do people compliment you on?

Here are mine to use as an example. I'm perpetually and sometimes annoyingly optimistic. I can find the lesson, the hope, the beacon of light that calls me forward. I've honed this gift; it helps me to navigate the uncertainty to innovate and create. It helps me to inspire others as a leader, parent, and a coach. However, I'm not blindly optimistic. If my house burned down, I wouldn't say, "Oh good, I didn't need that shit anyway." I know how to use optimism to move me forward.

I'm great at taking complex situations and framing them into simple terms, symbols, and metaphors. This gift is rooted in my love of writing that's been present since I was a child. I've honed this gift with years of interviewing and asking good questions. This made me a great listener. And the years as a consultant and salesperson helping clients see their problems and become hopeful about solutions continually refined this gift. I use this in all aspects of writing, speaking, coaching, parenting, and being a good friend.

I'm a connector. I connect people to each other, to their story and to the bottom line of their business. This is a combination of years of bartending, customer service, leadership, and being an only child and desperately wanting connection in my life. Now in my mid-fifties, I know this is my meaning and purpose bubbling to the top of years of what seemed like meaningless jobs and projects. All of those seemingly meaningless jobs and projects were introducing me to people and situations that help me see and know others well in all walks of life and all scenarios.

Dig deep when answering the question, "What are your unique talents?" I shared earlier about a client using her time as a leader on the soccer team, which was the same leadership skill she's using as an executive. When she shared that she loved soccer, I dug deeper. What was it about soccer that she loved? Was it the winning, the training, the team camaraderie? Dig into the essence of things as you explore yourself and what makes you *you*.

You may say you're great at marketing. What is it about marketing that you love? For some it's the creative storytelling; for others it's the metrics of customer buying behavior or the organization of activities that go into building a marketing plan.

I often discover my clients have migrated too far from their unique self as they've advanced in their careers. When we move too far from who we really are, we begin to feel a sense of dissatisfaction that we can't always identify. We just feel "off." What we're feeling is a striving battle of who we are and what we actually do every day. I believe this is a cause of burnout.

While working with Wendy, an executive director for a nonprofit, she had transformed the business from barely making it to heavily funded and expanding. In the midst of that growth she had veered away from her speaking talent, crafting the vision, and solving systemic problems, to more of an operational role. She shared with me, "I don't know how much longer I can do this." As we dug into her day-to-day work, it was clear she was no longer using many of her gifts. She was beginning to think she needed to find a new organization to lead. What she really needed was to align her responsibilities back to her talents and to do the same for her leadership team. Other people were better suited to the operational work, and she could get back out in front leading the organization. In a matter of months, she landed millions more in funding and launched solutions on a statewide and national platform. She's thriving again, and so is the organization.

What do people compliment you on? This one isn't as simple as it sounds. When we get complimented on something from our talents, we have a tendency to dismiss the compliment or possibly see it as disingenuous because our gifts are so innate that we dismiss them or think everyone has them. They don't. Pay attention to the compliments you receive.

To thrive, we use our talents to serve others. When we rely on our Inner Thrive Guide, we gain confidence. We stand taller, looking out over the horizon with curiosity to courageously explore what's next. And when we stand taller, others take notice and are inspired by our confidence and courage. It's time to bring your story into the world.

CHAPTER 6
Nobody Thrives Alone

Our work has the ability to heal our hearts when we connect our gifts and talents in relevant and impactful ways to work we know matters to another human. So much of our day-to-day work can be done in isolation. We can check everything off our list and get to inbox zero without knowing how our work matters to one another. Without intentionally acknowledging the connection of how our work serves another human, we won't derive a sense of well-being and thriving. When we show up having done the work to truly know ourselves, then go in search of people we can give our gifts to with kindness and generosity, that's the real deal.

Those with satisfying relationships and connections are healthier, happier, and longer lived. In his book *Social: Why Our Brains Are Wired to Connect*, Matthew Lieberman uncovers the neuroscience behind connection.[17] In his TED Talk from 2013, he claims by being intentional about the need for social connection, we can be smarter, happier, and more productive. Our brains are constantly reading the minds of others for connection.[18] To be intentional about our connection and find "our people" requires investing in our own personal reflection. Knowing ourselves first helps to send the signals to those who are our puzzle connector pieces. Whom do we serve, and who serves us?

Vulnerably exploring and acknowledging our uniqueness prepares us for empathy and kindness. When we know ourselves and our intricacies we can show up authentically to connect to say, "I'm here, I'm aware, and I'm ready to serve and work together." Consistently standing tall in our own story shows others they can trust us because we're willing to be exactly who we are. And when we pay the price to overcome the uncertainty to be our unique, messy, genuine selves, we more naturally experience empathy for others and their individuality.

To compare is to drop our gifts and talents into a dark, dusty corner in the pursuit of the gifts not meant to be ours. Stealing the gifts of others in comparison robs us the joy of our innate uniqueness. Instead of the deep pull to compete and compare, let us stand in awe, mesmerized with appreciation for each of our stories.

In a 2018 survey on loneliness conducted by Dr. Douglas Nemecek, chief medical officer for behavioral health at Cigna, stated, "Loneliness has the same impact on mortality as smoking fifteen cigarettes a day, making it even more dangerous than obesity."[19] In a time when we have more access to travel, social media, and communication tools, we are dying from loneliness and lack of connection. Not only is connection critical to thriving, we don't really survive without it. We weren't taught connection as a part of our early education process, and now we're suffering.

Helping Isn't Cheating

School tells you to keep your eye on your own paper; you're graded and evaluated on your individual effort. We are shown during our most formative years that helping someone else is cheating. It's impossible for this idea not to become embedded into our story center, that helping and collaborating is a bad idea.

Schools have tried in recent years to incorporate group projects to encourage collaboration. They don't, however, teach how to work together on a project and appreciate how our differences work together. After years of being told not to work together, students are thrown into a group project. Often grades are still individual, so there's a mixed message. It's frustrating and not at all effective to have one or two of the group members typically doing all the work and resenting the others. This further fuels our perspective that working together is bad. That same dysfunction enters the workplace. It's no wonder millions of dollars are spent by organizations teaching employees and leaders about trust and collaboration. Our competitive upbringing of individual achievement isn't tapping into our deepest human needs to be unique and connect.

Let's model for our children the beauty and comfort in asking for help rather than believing life is a solo act performed with fierce independence. We're all so "inside our heads" that sometimes we create our own solitude. When that Little Bitch in our head tries to dictate, it's no wonder we struggle with loneliness and isolation. We're already dealing with the primal need for survival and we didn't learn collaboration in our formative years from our early education, so we become paralyzed. We can change this. Business has the power to create meaningful connection. We are humans serving humans, after all.

We're not supposed to know everything and have it all together. That's the description of those perfect shiny round marbles, the mark of striving. We puzzle pieces are stronger and more beautiful together. Let others derive joy from helping you. We find a sense of our own worth and value by helping and serving others. Often genuine connection is "buried under busy."

Each year as a part of my Rise & Thrive Experience, I host a big event called Stand Tall in Your Story where the women in Rise & Thrive take the stage to give a TED-like talk of their story. The first Stand Tall in Your Story event was a huge undertaking. The first of anything is a big deal. Buried in details for the event and still needing to write and practice my opening keynote, I was struggling. I'm a keynote speaker, no big deal, right? Wrong. My brain was mush. I was tired, and it's really hard to write your own stuff when it's so close to your heart.

I took a break to meet with some friends. First of all, me taking a break during such a huge project showed real growth on my part! During dinner, they asked about the event, how I was doing, what I needed—as good friends do. I looked across the table at my friend and business partner, Alex Perry, who works with me as a Thrive Guide for my company, WEthrive.live. She's a speaking coach and communication expert with her own business, Practically Speaking. I asked, "Hey, what are you doing after this? I'd love some help with my keynote." I said this sheepishly because I didn't want to "bother" her with my event. I assumed she was busy and had more important things to do than help me. And I'm still working through the twelve-step program for control freaks.

Much to my surprise, she said, "I can stay and help you. I'd love that." After the rest of the group left, we bellied up to the bar and got to work. We laughed, we cried, we clapped our hands. Seriously, we did all of those things because working together with complementary gifts and talents is beautiful connection. We spent hours writing my speech and talking through every detail.

Alex later revealed to me that her confidence grew because I asked her to help me. Because she knew this was something I could have done myself, it meant so much to her that I trusted her with my big event. My keynote was so much better because I asked for help. I got out of my own head, and the Little Bitch didn't get to sit at the bar. Alex gave me such amazing direction for the keynote; she affirmed what is great about me because she knows me and loves me. She brought out the best in what she knew I wanted to deliver. She held up the mirror to help me see me. I affirmed her talents by asking for help. And, our relationship grew stronger and more beautiful by working together. That's what puzzle pieces do when we put them together. They're beautiful and stronger when clicked together.

> We shouldn't rob someone else the joy of helping! This is how we bless each other. Learn to accept help as a gift, not a weakness.
>
> —Jenny Tod[20]

You won't connect with everyone. You're not meant for everyone.

It's the uniqueness of our puzzle pieces that finds connections. We can't move through the world looking to please and connect with everyone. Alissa Teal is a dear friend and Thrive Guide for my company WEthrive.live. She's one of fewer than six hundred people in the world certified by *the* Brené Brown to facilitate Dare to Lead workshops. Alissa brings energy into the room and into her words. She writes under the brand Always_the_Rebel. She inspires moms to stand tall in their stories, especially those stories that are painful and challenging.

When Badass meets Rebel, you know there will be a connection. Alissa and I have known each other professionally for decades. We lost touch for many years through changes in life but reunited after both going through divorce, the mother lode of struggle. Our struggle brought us back together and then our deep longing for God to heal our pain, a perfect example of the connections that will come to you when you need them if you allow yourself to be seen. Instead of hiding our pain, we connected and said, "Let's heal together."

Through a long-distance relationship we continuously connected over text and phone to support each other in prayer and purpose to find our way after losing a whole hell of a lot. Determined to not let our challenges take us down, our puzzle pieces were forever connected in a desire to let God lead us up and out. Neither of us would be whole today without the support and sometimes ass-woopin' of a friend who wants only the best for you.

When Alissa received the news she had been accepted into Brené's Dare to Lead facilitation program, we both cried and cheered. She had worked long and hard, not only acquiring the skills for her to be considered but also because she was a corporate trainer and not a therapist, so she was an outlier in the group. She spent hours late at night, after her two kids went to bed, gathering the info she needed to show her certifications and credibility. It seemed like a long shot, but prayerfully she heard she at least needed to try. And God delivered— she was accepted!

We talked before she went to the weeklong training, and she decided to show up as her complete self, not wearing the corporate mask we had both known so well. Since God had seen her worthy enough to give her the opportunity, she'd lean into her and talents. Alissa has an interior design background, a runaway gypsy spirit, and a look to go with it. We've had our share of laughs about the absurdity that people like us ended up successfully leading in corporate America. We didn't seem like likely candidates. Yes, we both have runaway stories—maybe we'll tell you in a future book!

During the weeklong training, each candidate had a picture taken for the Brené Brown website. On the day of pictures, Alissa was dressed like Alissa—not corporate Alissa, but the real authentic Alissa in a jean jacket and leopard print head wrap. Afterward she said to me, "Maybe I should have worn something more corporate? What if clients don't hire me because they don't think I'm serious?" We both agreed that if God put her in the room, He wasn't going to block her success based on her leopard head wrap. But these are the stories we make up as we swim in the Sea of Uncertainty.

Later, Alissa called me laughing. "Guess what?" she said. She was contacted by a large company to teach Dare to Lead. This was exciting enough but not the whole story. The client said as they scrolled through all the pictures, they came upon Alissa in her jean jacket and leopard headband and knew she was the one for them! Yes, she had the qualifications—no different than the six hundred others on the website—but what got her the job was her style.

When we allow ourselves to be seen for ourselves, we attract those we're meant to work with and be with. Conversely, when we attempt to hide, afraid of showing our style or inadequacies, we ultimately hide our gifts. We prevent those who need us from finding us.

When I started my podcast, I was advised the title Badass Women's Council might turn some people away. Luckily, my fellow Badass Women's Council founding member Emily Sutherland said, "Good. Those aren't your people." This is the power of true authentic connection, when others can hold up the mirror to help you reflect and honor your authentic self. It's through these connections we understand our value and relevance.

Connection over Control

Take both of your hands and make fists until your knuckles are white. Sit like that for a few moments. How does that feel? Stressful? Tiring? This is the feeling when we strive for control. Nothing gets in, nothing goes out.

Now open your hands like you're reaching out to receive something or give someone a high five or a hug. How does this feel? This is thriving connection. The giving and the receiving. But there's this other thing that might feel like connection but is a counterfeit and a trap. It's called "the fixer."

I'm a recovering "fixer." I always thought it was my job to prepare for every single possible challenge and to fix all the issues as they popped up, believing my organizational prowess was the solution to every problem.

I became a fixer while married to a man with ADHD and producing a son with the same diagnosis. I was the finder of all things, the planner of all things, and the fixer of all things. Most of my waking moments and even some of my sleeping ones were spent preparing, fixing, and being overly prepared for the next thing. I would multitask while doing everything: at home making dinner and thinking the best way to get things cleaned up and kids to bed, barely hearing the conversations taking place in the kitchen, or at work sitting in the client meeting thinking of the next three moves to make to be sure everything was under control.

I'm exhausted just thinking about it, but at the time it seemed like good use of my talents. I mean, God must have put a productivity consultant in a family with two guys with ADHD on purpose. This was my chance to be the superhero! And that is where it all starts to fall apart ... when you believe your role is to fix someone.

Unintended consequences happen from being a fixer. The first: when you jump in to fix someone, you imply they are broken. No one wants to feel broken. People are not here to be fixed. We fix things, like chairs and computers, not people. We control things like expenses and scrap material, not people. When we jump in to fix others, we've basically said, "You weren't good enough, or you weren't enough; your uniqueness is not valued." Being a fixer implies a hierarchy: I'm better than you, smarter than you, more organized than you. When we fix things for other people, we rob them of a part of their story, their struggle, their own solution. There are a lot of right answers to most challenges. Figuring things out is how we learn and grow. The final unintended consequence of being a fixer: the relationship is damaged.

Instead of the love and gratitude we expect as a reward for being a fixer, we're met with frustration. If we continue to fix and imply brokenness, even unintentionally, over time, there is resentment. This is heartbreaking because our intent was to be loving and kind and helpful. And when we're met with frustration, it's so terribly confusing. We say, "Don't you want my help? I'm only helping you because I care about you." This happens in families and with managers and leaders.

But was our intent really to be kind, loving, and helpful? Or was the underlying motive to move past the uncertainty and discomfort that things won't get done or they won't be done OUR way? The next time you are offering help to someone, ask yourself if you're being a fixer to make your life easier or more comfortable. Sometimes we jump in to fix and offer help because the solution doesn't look like we think it should, or maybe the person is in the midst of figuring it out and it's still messy. Because of the excessive value we place on control, we move through the world thinking things have to be fixed, including people. And because education told us there's one right and wrong answer, we believe our way is the RIGHT way.

Nope.

Our solutions to some of the same problems will be very different. When we jump in to fix someone with our answer as the only right answer, not only do we imply their brokenness, we step on their belief systems about themselves. We become an unintended villain in their story. We think we enter as the superhero to fix and save the day, yet we're seen as the enemy. In every epic story there is a great battle with the villain. We now know this battle as striving. And from the battle, the villain doesn't rise victorious.

> Once you villainize someone, there is nothing
> left to do but go to war with them.
> —REESE WITHERSPOON AS BRADLEY JACKSON[21]

Many teams I have worked with over the years were stuck and not making progress because the manager or the leader was exhibiting too much control and not letting others choose their way forward. When people know you will jump in to fix their work or override your choices, they'll no longer rise to a decision. They'll simply wait to be told what to do by the controlling boss.

The moral of the story—don't be a fixer. A fixer's goal is control, not connection. Instead, when faced with uncertainty, be kind, be curious, be connected. Best to observe, ask questions, and truly listen. Listen for what they are saying, feeling, and what they're not saying. Listen to hear their story, not fix or give advice. Listening helps people to talk through their challenges and often is the only help they need. The loving and kind act of listening says, "I care," and we tap into the greatest human need, to be seen, heard, and known. Listening is the power move for our humanity; it feeds our soul. Life is messy, but it's not always your job to clean it up. Stop getting in the way, trying to control the universe.

Community That Isn't Your Company

There's significant value in building a community of support outside of your organization. In fact, I recommend when seeking connection to start with people outside your company.

I intentionally went out and built my first community after leaving a nineteen-year career. As I was building a business as an entrepreneur, aka working alone, I realized not only did I need to find clients, but I also needed to find friends! All of my career friends were all over the world attached to my previous company and none down the street. Without the schedule of our work meetings and conferences, I knew we would struggle to maintain the same closeness.

So, I went looking for career women friends. I looked for clues from women who I thought might be wanting connection. A casual acquaintance posted on social media that she was also leaving her corporate career. I messaged, "Hey, want to have coffee and be freaked out together?" An immediate "YES!" Another contacted me looking for career advice, and I invited her in. Another was a connection from an Instagram conversation. One by one I asked if they'd like to gather once a month and support each other in our businesses. A collective "YES!" I scheduled our first meetup and flippantly called us The Badass Women's Council, having no idea how profound this would become in my story.

I wasn't sure what to expect. I only knew I needed people to support me in my life, those who understood how important my career is to my overall life and well-being. It was my gut feeling, my Inner Thrive Guide leading me. Before our first meeting I was as nervous as a seventh grader walking into a new school. *What if they don't like me? What if they don't like each other? What if they realize this was a really dumb idea?* I changed my clothes three times before that breakfast meeting. The Sea of Uncertainty was churning; this is forever a part of our lives.

Many ask me, "But *how* did you ask them to be a part of the community?" Another example where the Sea of Uncertainty stops us from doing the basic things we need and want. Even as grown women, we struggle with the vulnerability to invite someone into our life. *What if they don't like me? What if I don't like them?*

During the first meeting of The Badass Women's Council, many of the women didn't know each other, and yet, within minutes a sort of magic happened. We all recognized how much we needed this connection. It was a void we didn't know we had until we looked around the room and saw the faces of these women ready to step in and fill that space.

We had more differences among us than similarities in personality, politics, upbringing, and religion. The common connection was our deep desire for each and every one of us to achieve our career dreams. The first morning we shared our goals and our vulnerabilities. Uncertainty was a common theme. Not only did we cheer each other on, but we also offered resources, support, and introductions.

For more than four years now, The Badass Women's Council continues to cheer and support one another. We've had business collaborations, spirited conversations about strategy and ideas, and we've also experienced the loss of parents, divorce, and deep discussions about the intricacies of life. We've provided a month's worth of meals after a dad died or the exact referral needed for another's business. We don't always see things the same. We don't always agree. We have our squabbles and struggles, as humans do. But the intent is always, *Are you okay? How can I help you?* Like a loving and kind first responder in our lives.

The work I do today is helping busy career women build their own Badass Women's Councils because it's not enough to know ourselves or develop our own skills. We are social beings, and it's in the sharing and supporting that we find our true value and worth.

1. We need perspective and language outside of our own company. We can get trapped and a bit brainwashed by our organization. We tend to develop our own language and views from inside the bubble.

2. We need people supporting *our* career goals and dreams. Because the needs of a company are to control, measure, and optimize, when we're good at our role in the company, it wants us to stay in that role and continue to get better. As much as we say we want to develop our employees for growth opportunities, moving people into new positions is disruptive to the organization. The company invites you into new positions that fit the company needs first, not always aligned to your career desires. Having a community of support outside of your organization gives you the freedom to discuss your personal goals and dreams and to craft plans in making job changes and promotions that fit your needs.

3. A community isn't built on hierarchy like a team inside a business. There's no "boss" to the community. As we rise higher on the organizational chart of our company, our group of peers gets smaller and smaller. The higher in position for your company, the more you need a well-built community, one that doesn't report to you and isn't tied to your paycheck. The community is a place to test out new ideas simply by saying them out loud, voicing your insecurities without fear of the company losing confidence in your abilities. This builds your own psychological safety, confidence, and courage.

4. The network becomes your personal PR team. Imagine a group of six to eight high-achieving women out in your community looking for opportunities for you, recruiting for you, and overall representing your best self. This is the ripple effect of intentionally building a community.

Who in your life holds up the mirror to reflect your insane talent and worth back to you in a genuine way? Who are those you trust who affirm you in a way that builds your self-esteem and self-worth? Who sees you swimming the Sea of Uncertainty and calms your anxiety by reminding you of your worth and your truth? This is the power of intentionally building your community.

CHAPTER 7

Your Story Framework: Creating the Conditions to Thrive

Here it is! The framework to create the conditions for your personal story, with everything your brain is looking for to thrive. Move over Abraham Maslow and your outdated hierarchy of needs—there's a new way to illustrate our thriving human needs: personal, emotional, and social.

This is Your Story Framework, honoring your human needs. I've listed the six things your brain needs to honor personal reflection, social connection and the emotional flow of our lives.

Your Story Framework

Personal Reflection

Meaning

Social Connection

Purpose

Emotional

Food
Water
Rest
Energy

Self-Talk
Optimism
Faith
Stillness
Gratitude

Gifts
Talents
Abilities
Personality
Style

Psychological
safety
Emotions
Ideas
Mistakes

Giving and
receiving gifts
Generosity
Kindness

Value
Relevance
Impact

Reflection: an exercise done to determine your meaning.

Connection: where we go to serve a purpose to other humans, satisfying our need to live as social beings.

Like every great story, there is an emotional flow of highs and lows, trauma and drama, joy and celebration that exists in our story. We feel our way through life.

Our time in reflection determines our level of self-awareness, leading to self-love, self-respect, and self-confidence. This time with ourselves then sets us up for meaningful relationships, both personally and professionally. By investing in ourselves for reflection, we enter relationships healed and whole. Time spent in personal reflection builds a foundation for our quality of life and career. How much time are you spending in personal reflection now? I'm going to state it real plain and simple: without the time in reflection to know yourself well, you can't get to thriving; you'll be stuck striving. Without knowing yourself well, you can't build a life and write a story from your point of view. You'll always be at the mercy of someone else's opinions and expectations of you.

Reflection:

- How do I feel?
- What do I need?
- What do I want?
- What makes me *me*?
- What do I love about my work?

This gives our life meaning. This allows us to live authentically and genuinely. When someone asks, "Who do you think you are?" you'll know, wholeheartedly and unapologetically. Knowing ourselves well isn't an act of ego grandstanding; it's an act of service.

With reflection first, we build confidence in ourselves that then evokes the courage to have more natural curiosity about the stories of others. We're bolder. We have less of a need to defend ourselves or compare. With an investment in reflection, we can disagree, be wrong, make mistakes, and learn and grow from the exchange, still confident in ourselves and in our abilities. We can grow from our relationships to adapt and learn.

Connection:

- Is this a safe place for me to be me?
- Is this a safe place for my ideas, my mistakes, and my emotions?
- Who am I here to serve with my gifts and talents?
- How am I valuable and relevant to other humans?

We don't earn our meaning and purpose with a degree or a certification. We don't pick it up as a glass award on the stage from the CEO at the banquet. We discover it and uncover it. We own it. Our Inner Thrive Guide carries it with us wherever we go. The conversation around meaning and purpose has taken on such a grandiose, bigger-than-life expectation. It feels like a literal mountain we must climb on some inspired day near the end of our lives to find this nicely wrapped package marked "meaning and purpose" perched under a sign saying "You Are Here." We stand on that mountaintop and look out over the clouds with awe and wonder as we miraculously determine we're here to cure cancer or solve inner city hunger so our lives are finally worth the years of striving. Doesn't that seem like unachievable bullshit?

I prefer a more pleasing perspective that our meaning and purpose can be found in the day-to-day of our entire lives and that it grows and evolves, honoring the ages and stages of our life. I love seeing my life as a story that unfolds chapter by chapter as my curiosity leads me down a bread crumb trail of discovery, eager for what's next. Knowing each chapter of our story is rich with meaning keeps us from the pull to compare and contrast our stories with envy and frustration. We're free to live the chapter we're in. And when we hit those chapters of struggle and frustration, we can take comfort knowing it's a chapter, not our entire story. We take the lessons from the struggle and begin to write a new chapter.

When using reflection and connection to find meaning and purpose in our careers, we're not focused on the title, salary, industry, or our company achievements; we're asking how we want to feel in the day-to-day work. We're looking to use our individuality intentionally to serve other humans, and in return we feel valuable and relevant.

Maybe you're starting out fresh on your career journey. That's great! We need your fresh perspective of the work, the company, and the world around us. Your fresh perspective could be the value you provide to others in this chapter. Follow the bread crumb trail of discovery, picking up little nuggets you chew on a bit before moving on to the next. No need to push for the title or the promotion too soon. You're looking to be valuable and relevant. The achievements and promotions will come from your contribution.

Or you could be feeling buried and exhausted, trying to dig out of a mountain of other people's expectations, unsure of who you are underneath it all. Your discovery will be chipping away and discarding the pieces that don't fit, like a carver revealing the masterpiece of your story deep within you.

Maybe you're thriving in a career where you know exactly who you are and wake up each day eager to deliver your gifts generously. YES! We need as many of you as possible in our companies and leading commerce in society. Buy your team copies of this book, lead them, and encourage them to find their talents. Tell your story and give them the space of psychological safety to curiously explore while you guide them and cheer for them.

Daniel Pink in his book *Drive* shares the research on the drivers for living a great story: autonomy, mastery, and purpose. He defines autonomy as the need to direct your own life and work. To be fully motivated, you must be able to choose what you do, when you do it, and who you do it with. This is our personal story. According to Pink, autonomy motivates us to think creatively without needing to conform to strict workplace rules. He goes on to say that those motivated by autonomy seek mastery, the desire to improve.[22]

When we're interested in something, good at something, and know how it matters to another human, we want to practice continually and get better. We keep looking for additional pieces to the puzzle to connect to reveal the bigger, stronger, beautiful picture.

Purpose is the belief we're working on something bigger than ourselves. When we bring our distinct self to serve another human we *are* working on something bigger than ourselves. Working to connect and serve another human being is thriving. It's in that beautiful puzzle of connection we want to get better, learn more, and connect our pieces.

This concept doesn't require us to be more intelligent than another, more creative than another; this isn't about competition and comparison—it's about uniqueness and connection. Humans need to know they matter. The gifts of a scientist working on a treatment to cure cancer aren't better than the daycare worker who nurtures children; they're just different. Human-to-human serving, providing value and relevance.

Paying the price to intentionally write our story while honoring the struggles required to cross the Sea of Uncertainty causes empathy for others to surface naturally. A true appreciation for our own journey evokes a curiosity and an appreciation for another's story and journey. Comparison becomes less prevalent, less important; instead, we focus on connection.

CHAPTER 8
Connection: Your Company Story

We bring our personal story into the company story. We're not coming into the company to "prove ourselves"; we're coming to add value, relevance, and impact. We come bearing our God-given gifts learned from a lifetime of our experiences. By continually doing the work of reflection, we know ourselves well and we honor our uniqueness like a gift wrapped in beautiful paper and bows, ready to be given with kindness and generosity. We're not asking the company for permission to be valuable—that's striving, battling for our worth. We come ready to make a difference to grow the company we've chosen to serve in. It is our duty to find a company where our personal story is respected and valued. Because you've done the work in reflection to be intensely self-aware, you know your worth and the value you bring into a company.

What is a company story? Well, it's a human story, because business is human. A company story depicts the value we provide to each other, human to human. A company story involves all the employees, customers, suppliers, and even the families associated with all of the humans that work for a company. A great company writes the company story so clearly that every employee knows the customer they serve, what problems they solve for those customers, and why it matters.

A company story is where you bring your personal story to work each day. We all have responsibility in the company story. Start by asking several questions: What conditions do you work best in? Where are you taking your gifts each day? Consider the amount of direction you prefer, the style of manager, the flexibility, and the work environment where you thrive. Dig deep to know these things. Don't leave it up to chance.

These questions often challenge my clients. It could be partially because they've never considered that they have the power to affect the conditions they work in, instead simply accepting whatever comes with the title. We spend a third of our life at work, more if we count commute times. The type of environment and conditions we work in affect the other 70 percent; we don't have two lives, one for work and one for a career life. We have *a* life. We spend nearly the same percentage of our life sleeping. Would you tolerate a terrible mattress and sleeping with no pillows? Or would you create the conditions for a better night's sleep?

Once you have identified the conditions you work best in, seek them in your company story and create them. Ask for what you need, take the breaks you need, and take your work to the space that inspires or calms you. Most organizations now have far more freedom of choice in working conditions. I find with many clients that even when their organization gives them choices about the working conditions, their pull to the old habits of being caught up, always trying for more, and proving themselves are the bigger barriers to taking lunch breaks, breathing breaks, and setting personal boundaries for their work hours.

Maybe you need to make a company change to create better conditions for yourself. Opportunities are out there. Tenure on its own isn't a measure of success. The years of service awards for most organizations aren't all that compelling. Are you sticking around for ten years in a job that sucks the life out of you for a gold watch or another week's vacation? Dear Lord, buy your own watch and move on. Likely you stay because the uncertainty of making a change is too great, and you say things like, "It's not that bad. I've been here this long. I can stick it out. The benefits are good." This is like playing a game not to lose instead of playing to win.

I hope you're in a career that rewards and challenges you for many years. I've had that experience. It's rich and gratifying. It can also feel like a trap. Once you're in an organization so deep that you can't imagine working anywhere else, this is the time to reflect and become really aware and intentional. The comfort zone can ensnare you.

- Are you still growing?
- Are you still adding value?
- Are you comfortable?
- Too comfortable?

Comfortable is the beginning of complacent, which also can be the decline of your self-worth and possibly the decline of your value to the company. Do yourself and the company a favor; jump into the Sea of Uncertainty and find something that lights you up again, either within the same organization or in a new company. New jobs and new industries are popping up far quicker than ever before in our history, largely due to the internet, so there is opportunity. Most companies have done away with pensions guaranteeing your financial security; is a slight match on 401K enough to stay, or can you own your own investment strategy?

I met with a woman in a career so toxic that it was borderline abuse. All of her ideas were being shut down daily by the owner of the company. I listened to her story, searching for a reason why she would possibly stay in this environment. She's bright, talented, and articulate. It made no sense. I simply asked, "Why do you stay?"

She had changed companies within the same industry four times over a fifteen-year period. Two companies ago, while in a meeting, a former boss made a comment that she had worked in a lot of places. This comment haunted her, and she believed she had to stay with a company, any company, for many years to overcome this "problem." I couldn't help but be curious. I asked about her relationship with this former boss. He had not been a good leader to her or anyone else in the organization. They no longer spoke and hadn't for years.

"So, you're making long-term career choices based on a seven-year-old comment made by a man you don't even like enough to invite to a barbecue in your backyard?" I asked her. After a long pause and a slow *blink*, she said, "Yes, and it has to stop."

If we're feeling disconnected from the company story, it is our responsibility to take our gifts and find one where we can continue to serve. Know yourself so well that you can advocate for your career growth. This is why accepting you're afraid daily is key to growth. Evolving puts us in situations we've never been in before. But too often we stunt our own growth by being uncomfortable with change and therefore unwilling to pack up our gifts and move them.

Take back your power and your story. Know yourself and your industry so well that you are never a hostage to a narrative that is not from your own voice. With the vast number of career choices available today, either working for someone else or creating your own opportunities, there is no reason to work for assholes and allow them to get into your head and inform your future.

The upcoming chapters talk about money. Being paid well is important but second in line to our primary objective to bring our personal story into a company story where we are safe to be human, where we can learn, grow, and be ourselves and make a difference. The coming chapters also show you how to increase your value by knowing the money-making model of the business. When we choose a career for money before story, that's striving, and it's been happening for decades. That needs to stop.

Knowing the value and relevance of our daily work is how we find meaning in the day-to-day of our lives. The really great news is that you don't need a leadership title to show people how they matter in the day-to-day work. We can show this with affirmation and gratitude to our coworkers, customers, and suppliers. We are humans serving humans. We can show up to work with our human needs front of mind. We can honor the personal, emotional, and social needs of those we work with and serve each day.

My friend Liesel Mertes is a workplace empathy consultant. The fact we need workplace empathy consultants shows a real gap in our education and business practices and our neglect of acknowledging our human needs. Liesel experienced such a wide variety of responses while trying to return to work after the loss of her child that she decided to teach others what empathy looks and sounds like. Somehow when people get into the office, they lose their confidence and ability to act as humans. Humans need love, empathy, and connection. The deepest human need is to be seen and heard and known. This is a 24/7 need, not one reserved for after the workday has ended.

You don't need an organization chart to get to know someone as a human in your company. As a sales executive in a large organization, I knew that many people touched the work that I sold. Even though we didn't report to the same leaders or work on the same team, I made it a point to get to know them, what they loved about their job, and what made it difficult. I asked how I could align the work I sold to help them. I didn't wait for permission to look for ways to optimize our work together.

At the end of the year, I wrote an email to all of the consultants who had worked on projects with me that year. I thanked them and told them how their work helped me and what I appreciated about each of them. This wasn't an assignment from human resources with a box to be filled out. It wasn't a form letter; it was a human thank-you note from one hard-working professional to another, saying, *I see you, thank you,* and *you matter.* The more I connected in a human way to my colleagues, the easier it was to get work done and the more we showed up for one another—in good times and especially in the tough times.

In fact, these work relationships became a part of my life story. Again debunking the whole life-balance bullshit: one life, not two. During my divorce when my life was a complete shit show and I could barely do my job, I was struggling emotionally, my sales were in the toilet, and so was my paycheck. A colleague reached out to me and said, "My wife and I talked last night. We see your sales are down and we know you're struggling. We have $5,000 here you can tap into anytime you need it." I tear up just thinking about it. Human to human, we showed up for each other. We are not work humans and personal humans; we are just humans.

The organizational chart rules most companies. This is a part of control, measure, optimize. Separate the work into pieces and parts that are easier to manage. When striving, we look for what box we're in and what box we want to climb into next. The actual work, however, doesn't get done within those little boxes on the org chart; the work gets accomplished *across* the organization. Whatever department you work in, there's something that happens before you from another department's little box on the chart and after your part of the work. You and your department could have the best relationships, host birthday parties for coworkers, and at the same time isolate yourself in a little bubble of bliss from everything else going on in the organization. This is also striving, battling for our peace and trying not to interact with those outside our team. What if we could zoom out and see it differently? What if you could see yourself as a part of a relay track team working across the organization human to human instead of a name in a box on the org chart?

What's the most important aspect of a track relay team? The handoff. Each runner has a specific leg of the race, and it's the handoff between the runners that makes or breaks the race. The same is true for our work inside an organization. The greatest opportunity to remove waste and mistakes is in the handoff from department to department. Yet there isn't much effort put into the communication of how our work gets handed off from department to department, human to human.

If you want more influence and to improve your value in the organization, get to know the players on your relay team. Who are the people from other departments that hand you work, and where do you hand it over to when yours is completed? Do you know them as a human or an email address?

It doesn't matter how fast you run your part of the race if the handoff doesn't go well. In fact, on a relay track team, if the handoff doesn't go well, there are two consequences: one, you'll probably lose the race, and two, you'll have a hard time trusting your running partner the next time you run together. If you're the coach of a relay track team, if there's a missed handoff and a drop of the baton, you won't have that team running in the next practice. You'll have them practicing their handoffs. Are you practicing the handoff with your relay team partners with department-to-department meetings or lunches to get to know one another?

The more you know about the human challenges and opportunities in the departments that interact with yours, the better the handoff will go. When we wait for information to go up and down the organization, it slows things down and leaves room for truckloads of miscommunication. Look for opportunities to connect with people from other parts of the organization, ask them what's challenging about their work, how you could be more helpful in the handoff.

For example, if you're the manager of the service department, you don't need permission to go and build a relationship with the director of sales. So often we have conflicting priorities that we're unaware of, or the communication gets so convoluted by the time it goes up and down the organizational chart and back to us. And it bears noting that when we know the actual human and not just the email address, we work differently to meet their needs. I don't care if they are on the other side of the world—that's what technology is for—find a way to talk face-to-face and get to know them and their story.

When we go to work each day battling a company story that isn't aligned to our gifts and talents, or when we don't value our customer or the problems the company solves, this is striving. When a company story is unclear or toxic by nature, and we daily tolerate a bad boss or feel unsafe with our thoughts and ideas, this is striving. When we go to work each day and have no idea if our work matters, this is striving or maybe even just surviving. Thriving is different. We take responsibility to know ourselves and how our work matters to other humans.

Thriving is about growth, for us and for the company we serve. Sometimes through the process of this growth, our personal story and the company story no longer align. This was my story. For nearly two decades I was growing and thriving inside an organization where I was passionate about my work. I knew how and why my work mattered, and I was paid exceptionally. Then I noticed the company strategy was shifting, and with these changes I recognized my talents were not going to be nearly as meaningful in the next chapters of the company story. It was up to me to find a place where I could continue to grow and innovate. So I gave my notice. No shame, no shade, no frustration with the company. This was simply a misalignment in my story to the company story and my responsibility to recognize and adapt appropriately. We create the conditions for thriving in our personal story. Go back and underline that last sentence so you don't forget.

Thriving isn't waiting on permission from our boss to grow; it's knowing ourselves and the company story so well that we ask for the opportunities we want and need. Sometimes we can even create a role to align our value and impact to what the company needs. When we relinquish our growth completely to the company and wait for permission, we take the pen of writing our story out of our hands and put it into the hands of someone else. That's striving.

I recently worked with a client and she realized she wasn't using her gifts, talents, and abilities as intentionally as she'd like. I asked her how she could be using them more boldly. She recognized a legitimate need in her company that her gifts could solve. I helped her write a business case for creating this role, with both the value it would provide to the employees as well as the money-making model. She's working with her leadership to create this new position.

We're All Telling the Company Story

We're all participating in the company story. It's the conversations over dinner, the direct messages during and after a shitty meeting, the coffee klatches with our friends. This is why it's so important for leaders to be clear and include intentional context about the company story—because we all have our own interpretations of a message. A company story isn't controlled; it's told. Sorry, corporate communications and the executive team, we're all involved. For it to evolve and include all the humans, it's a leader's number one responsibility to create a safe place for the tough discussions about challenges and mistakes, to clarify understanding, and to truly listen to what people are saying and feeling.

Safety at work isn't only about the handrail on the stairs and well-marked fire exits. The term is *psychological safety*. Amy Edmondson, professor of leadership and management at Harvard School of Business, resurged the concept of psychological safety that had been discussed as early as the 1960s. Edmondson found baffling data showing the highest performing teams weren't those with the least mistakes; they were the ones with the most mistakes. She dug deeper to discover that the high-performance teams had created an environment where it was safe to pitch ideas and make mistakes. Originally, kindness was thought to be a key to high-performing cultures. But kindness—especially in a culture steeped in insincere compliments and patronization—keeps people from sharing mistakes or bad news.[23]

Here's the simple truth: our thoughts and emotions, fears and mistakes are fundamental elements in our ability to thrive at work and at home. The need for psychological safety is as basic as food, water, and shelter. Our mental health is as important as our physical health. Are we putting as much time, energy, and effort into our emotional well-being? Are we really keeping each other safe?

We can't bring our best decisions and innovations if we don't feel safe, including about our insecurities and mistakes. To live and work together in a beautiful, human way is to acknowledge the need to feel and to mess up. When we feel safe with our emotions, not only can we make better decisions for ourselves, but we also can create psychological safety for others. Yet we aren't encouraged to use our emotions at work. They are uncertain and impossible to control and measure; therefore, they aren't valued. We lose our ability to do great work trying to suppress our emotions.

Because humans are by nature uncertain, a leader recognizes the need to provide assurance. Without this, employees do not bring their full commitment to the company. There's no easy button for this; it takes the intention of leaders and managers willing to be vulnerable and empathic, to ask questions, and then to listen for what people are saying and feeling, clarifying through two-way communication. Communication of the company story isn't an email. It's a conversation. Connection over control.

As any new strategy, shift in direction, or recovery of a client problem is discussed, it requires space and grace, not sending an email and moving on. Human-to-human conversation is the role of a leader. Without inviting full human interaction into the story, you'll get, at best, compliance. Hire people with an appreciation and love for humans in both their mindset and their skills as your top priority. Things like vulnerability, transparency, empathy, and listening. We're now in the Age of Humanity; we speak human, interact human. The industrial age, where we pretend to control people and speak machine and ego, is dying.

Your Company Story Is Social

In today's world of social media, the company story is also being told by the employees and customers. The day has passed when the leaders control the company narrative. Now our role is to tell a very simple story of value and impact and invite each of our employees and our customers into the story.

In today's environment, trying to control the narrative can backfire. College student and paint store part-timer Tony Piloseno learned this the hard way. He used his passion for his job to create TikTok videos aimed at a much younger audience than the company's traditional marketing strategy. His approach drew in 1.2 million followers to his TikTok account @tonesterpaints, a play on his name and his personal brand. Tony bought the supplies himself, but because he was using company equipment, the nationwide paint company fired him for misuse of company property. The ramifications of the negative publicity with his young demographic of followers could affect its business long-term, even after those young people forget the exact reason why they have a negative impression of the brand.[24]

This is a great example of what not to do and is what happens when a company values control over connection. Consider what would have been possible had the company partnered with Tony funding an ad campaign for his account and capitalizing on his 1.2 million followers. This could have been a triumphant thrive story, personal story, company story, and the money-making model coming together to flourish. Instead, the company said to over one million humans, "Hey, that guy Tony you like who uses our products, we don't value him." Those that value Tony then disassociate with the company because they've wronged someone they followed and respected. In a beautiful twist, Florida Paints hired Tony and are fully embracing his personal story as a Sales Associate and Video Content Creator. You can learn more about the rest of Tony's story at tonestorpaints.com. He's found a company story that is fully embracing his passion and talent.

Speak Human. "Corporate Speak" Needs to Die.

In 2004, Jeff Bezos, CEO of Amazon, banned bullet points and PowerPoint in leadership meetings, replacing them with two-to-six-page reports. These narratives are submitted prior to the meeting for the leadership team to sit in silence reading for the first thirty minutes. To prepare a narrative, you must know your topic well and its context. This change forced leaders to prepare for meetings with greater diligence and then to more fully understand the story at the beginning of a meeting, not spend hours lazily browsing through bullet points, charts, or graphs.[25] Speak human, write, and tell the story.

The ability to tell stories through the eyes and ears of a human is a powerful skill for leaders. Talking in the shortcut language of acronyms and buzzwords has been a part of our work since the early 1900s. Emma Green's article in *The Atlantic*, "The Origins of Office Speak," reads like a mix of Dilbert cartoons and the *Wall Street Journal* and depicts the history and the humor of the words we use at work.

Over time, different industries have developed their own tribal vocabularies. Some of today's most popular buzzwords were created by academics who believed that work should satisfy one's soul; others were coined by consultants who sold the idea that happy workers are effective workers. The Wall Street lingo of the 1980s all comes back to "the bottom line," while the techie terms of today suggest that humans are creative computers, whose work is measured in "capacity" and "bandwidth." Corporate jargon may seem meaningless to the extent that it's best described as "bullshit," but it actually reveals a lot about how workers think about their lives.[26]

You may have noticed the theme of etymology throughout this book. I became maniacal about the words I chose. I want simple and intentional words that speak to a seventh grader or a Wall Street CEO. My desire is to create connection by grounding ourselves in the definition of these words and their true intent. This is important because we've become both lazy and egotistical with our words. Corporate speak: so many words, so many egos.

I spent much of my career in airports. You want to sit in the midst of a corporate-speak fest, go to the airport. Listen in to all the loud talkers closing their gaps, circling back, not having the bandwidth, getting their ducks in a row, and really focusing on those KPIs. In full disclosure, I helped contribute to this ocean of corporate speak, you know, the ocean we can't boil.[27] (Insert eye roll here referencing one of the most overused corporate phrases.) If I'm honest, I liked this corporate speak. Using it helped me feel a part of something, a kinship with smart people focused on doing good work. The consultant world became my "bubble" where I lived and worked. I'm not down on consultants; I'm down on consultant speak. I don't want to live in a bubble or to create a bubble that needs to be controlled and maintained. I want to live in curiosity to explore our human connection.

When I left my corporate job, it took nearly two years to purge the language of my previous company. This was a barrier I hadn't anticipated, one that made it difficult to get to the heart of what I believed, how I wanted to live and work, who I was in my own words. I am so grateful for my previous companies and the experience and relationships I gained—these were a true gift. Because our words have power, I needed to let go of those old words and really dig deep into my heart and discover who I was without their language, what was deeper than those word habits. Where was I in the midst of it all? This became the origin of my own coaching work to help clients identify their personal story first, then their company story. Knowing ourselves first allows us to shift from company to company without losing our sense of self.

For company leaders, my advice is always "If you can't hand it to a seventh grader and have them understand what you're trying to convey, it's not simple enough." To unify humans, we need a simple, joyful story. As much as corporate speak can create tribal connections, it can also be a barrier that creates uncertainty.

The two magical words for company story are *clarity* and *context*. Sound familiar? The deepest human need is to be seen and heard. Clarity isn't a presentation slide or a revenue goal. Clarity is a human narrative involving the emotions of humans. And to give clarity to what we are trying to accomplish or what needs to happen, we need context.

Context comes from Latin origin and means "to weave together."[28] In business, context is about weaving together the humans in your company. Clarity and context must come through in the story of what we're trying to accomplish, how the company has arrived at the goals and the strategy, and why it matters to all the humans involved.

These are magical words to use in your career. "Can you give me a little more clarity on this goal or this project?" A completely reasonable request. Or "Can you give me a little more context about these goals? They look great; I just want to understand more about how we got here and where it's taking us."

Company Story Framework

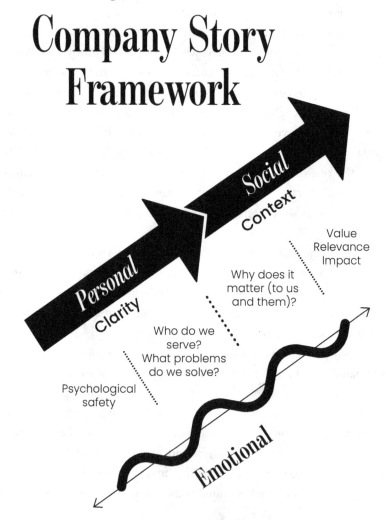

Story, Then Money

A business uses goals and metrics to unify the humans to let them know if they're winning or losing. The metrics tie to the money-making model of the business. A responsible business will control, measure, and optimize the money-making model.

Humans, though, need connections with each other. We glean this through stories. Because business is conducted by and for humans, our human needs should come first. We can't have a business without humans, so story first, then money. Both critical, yet the order matters. Money fuels our stories. Meaning and money are the power combo. Books like *Do What You Love and the Money Will Follow* by Marsha Sinetar suggest that when we build our work around our meaning and purpose, we produce a multiplier effect on our earning potential.[29]

The industrial age model has been money first, then story, governed by control and measured by size and achievement creating a conflict. Attempting to meet human needs with money first is striving. The Age of Humanity is now. Story first, then money, governed by connection and measured by human impact—that is growing, prospering, and thriving.

A team with a goal to increase sales from $3 million to $5 million by December 31 could rally and achieve the goal and then gather to celebrate with go-cart racing and cold beer while waiting to be told "what's next" without a real understanding of the difference they made to other humans—that's just celebrating achievement. Winning is great, celebrating is important, but in life, so is losing if we're looking through the lens of impact versus accomplishment.

When we lose, we learn. We can reflect on what needs to be changed to put us on a path to making a greater difference to the humans we serve. Story gives us an emotional attachment to the goal. When we miss a goal, this means we didn't serve the humans the goal was intended to serve. It's not just about missing the quarterly targets and the numbers on a spreadsheet. Sometimes the risk we take that leads to a loss is exactly what we needed to learn and progress. We'll look at the key of money next.

Consider this fictional example of a story told with clarity and context about a company making industrial cleaning supplies used in companies like schools and hospitals:

When we increase our sales from $3 million to $5 million this year, we will bring products to approximately five thousand more hospital patients, keeping the patients safe and allowing them to heal quickly without the risk of deadly infections. When our products are the best quality and properly labeled, our customers have the confidence we're here to serve them in their daily work.

Not only does this bring us rich satisfaction as human beings helping and serving others, we as employees of ACE Cleaning Company enjoy the benefits of keeping our own families secure and provided for with a safe and clean environment, competitive pay, and ample opportunities to learn and grow. Thank you for bringing your unique talents to this mission. Thank you for your ideas and your input to achieve this goal swiftly with our money-making model stable so we're financially ready to take on the next mission to serve. There will always be patients who need us to show up with quality products that keep their schools and hospitals clean and safe for our loved ones.

If you worked in this organization, you'd understand how the company affects humans, and you'd know why the money matters. It's then your responsibility to find connection from your work to that story.

I learned about the need for having a story with clarity and context while working on a team building the implementation process for the book *The 4 Disciplines of Execution*, a best-selling field guide for executives to run their business more effectively by reliably executing their strategic plans, an amazing approach to control, measure, and optimize.[30]

I was on a team in the early days, doing the work with clients to implement this four-step process. The process was simple and excruciatingly difficult at the same time. Simple in format but excruciating to align ten, five hundred, or sometimes five thousand humans and their individual stories and desires to a common strategy. Imagine this: a leader announces the grand strategy designed to progress the organization, and every person in the organization sees this strategy through the lens of their story. Every person is riddled with uncertainty and looks for ways NOT to have to change the way they do their work. This is the part of leadership that keeps executives up at night. What if employees won't execute the plan? Numerous strategies are mapped out in documents stuck in a laptop or on flip chart pages that get thrown into the trash, strategies that would have worked if people would have just rallied around the plan. Many successful leaders realized it wasn't a better strategy they needed—it was an execution plan. Brilliant.

While breaking the strategy down into the execution plan is a great improvement to business to control, measure, and optimize, a key difference emerged between my clients that got exceptional results and those that struggled.

You know where I'm going with this, right? The difference was in the story. The leaders who saw the execution framework as a way to get employees to do what they were told and be compliant, like parts on the assembly line, experienced pushback and, in some situations, revolt. You see, people smell your intent before you open your mouth. If the intent is only to improve the numbers, the humans aren't all that interested. If the intent is to serve humans in some way, well, now you have their attention.

When goals are established and scoreboards posted with no compelling story to invite humans into participate, you'll get some compliance but not real connection. *Hey team, let's rally to increase revenue from $3 million to $5 million by December 31! Yay team, go team, let's take that big hill!* That's the rallying cry of a leader trying to improve a number, not engage humans.

A goal isn't a story. Do we set goals in our company? Absolutely. They are critical to unify the team. Measurable goals are critical. But goals must come with a story. The goal gives clarity; the story gives context for why it matters to humans.

Goals alone leave way too much room for assumption and interpretation without the story's compelling context. We are not machines here to produce. We are beautiful humans looking for value and relevance. When we see how we can add value, we bring our finest diligence and effort. You won't have to bring big cookies to the meeting, set up foosball tables in the breakroom, or threaten to cut off our bonus if we don't perform. With a compelling connection from our story to the company story, we pull out all the stops to win because we're serving, helping, and connecting.

I spent decades of my life standing on ugly carpeting under bad lighting. You know the rooms I'm talking about? Large ballrooms of a swanky hotel full of mostly middle-age dudes from all over the world. Large flip chart pages lined every wall, scribbled in ink that smells weirdly like fruit ... no idea why that became a thing. From the middle of the room, if you didn't have the context that this was a business meeting, these pages with their colors, lines, and symbols without using full words, only acronyms, resembled a Wassily Kandinsky painting. Kandinsky is a Russian painter, a pioneer in abstract art. Abstract is not what we're going for in a business discussion. With each chart scribbled with the grand plan and the gap closure and the SWOT analysis and the metrics and the process and the value proposition—in these meeting rooms we stopped speaking our native language of the human story and started to speak machine. What's missing in each of these corporate meeting room billboards is why any of this shit matters. Who cares? Where is the human emotional connection? Without context, each of us fills in the blanks with our own assumptions, and each of the stories we make up are different enough to not bring the clarity and unity we desire for the company's goals and strategies.

I walked around the room taking notice of those teams that were just bitching and moaning versus those that seemed interested and engaged. I asked the teams to stand up and gather in small groups. Just standing up tells our brains we're actual humans, not droids assigned to a table like parts of a machine.

I asked the groups to stand together and tell the story of why these goals mattered. At first I got the look of "Who is she again? Why are we telling stories? Don't we have work to do?" I persisted. Often my persistence netted better results than my intelligence. I didn't always know the right answer immediately. I trusted my inner thrive guide to stay curious, ask questions, listen, learn, fail, try again. If I'm honest, I may have actually been buying time trying to figure out how to turn this shit show into something worthy of the invoice they would be receiving for my work that day. Slowly they began to talk to each other. I walked around the room listening for clues. I wasn't sure what I was listening for other than "Does anyone know why this matters?"

The pattern began to emerge. The CEO told why these goals mattered. He spoke of the meaningful impact this work would have to the customers and their communities. He spoke of the way this plan would allow the company to serve and grow. He told the story of humans and how they would benefit, the employees, the customers, and the communities they lived and worked in. People in his group were leaning in, some mesmerized by this new clarity and context and the human element involved in the strategy.

The teams furthest away from the CEO in geography and on the org chart didn't have the same "lean in" effect. In fact, those groups were mostly complaining and not really trying to fulfill my request of telling the story of why their flip chart hieroglyphics mattered. They were arguing about the validity of the data and the metrics. This is what happens when we don't have context.

Those who know the story are more engaged. Leaders who understand the power of the human story have more winning teams. The ability to stay connected through story is the responsibility of everyone in a business, not just the CEO. Seeking the human connection of our work gives us all more value and more meaning.

I've listened to more leaders speak than most people I know, based on my years of standing in these swirly carpeted rooms. I've heard the well-dressed executive with the soothing tone and his fancy words be described as "captivating," and then those same people get in the elevator after the speech and say to each other, "He's great, but I have no idea what that meant." I'm not making this up.

Creating a story spoken clearly in simple human terms, real words, not corporate speak, describing the characters and how they connect: this is our job as leaders, as parents, as community builders. It's not actually about winning or losing from the scoreboard of goals and measurements. The goals and measurements must tell the story of how achieving the goal will make a difference to a human. It's not the winning that provides the connection—it's the reason why the goal matters at all. We won't curb burnout from more control and achievement, only through working with more human connection through the power of our stories.

PART II
Money

CHAPTER 9
Money Stories

Money. Just reading the word evokes a vibe, an emotion, an opinion. I'm not a financial advisor, a banker, or an expert investor. I'm here to talk about money as an essential foundation of life. We must discuss it to thrive. Many of our striving ways stem from perspectives about money that create a conflict in our heads and our hearts. We need to talk very clearly about money, without flinching. There's no shame in acknowledging the importance of money.

We unlock the door to growth with the key to our story first, then use the key of money to unlock prosperity. Money is a necessary and neutral commodity. Necessary because we can't function without it and neutral because money on its own isn't good or bad—it just is. We give money its value through our perspectives about it. The topic comes with more dysfunction and strife than politics and religion. We don't discuss it enough using the practical role money plays in life and business. Let's change that. Let's get started looking at both our personal money stories and the role the money-making model plays to be more valuable and relevant in our careers.

I feel some of you rolling your eyes. Honestly, this is a part of the problem. Let's break it down. What is prosperity? It's not just about money. Prosperity is the condition of being strong and sustainably successful in heart, mind, and your bank account. *Prosper*, which comes from the Latin word *prosperare*, is to be in the condition of thriving. And great news, we create our conditions for thriving. We decide what prosperity means to us. We decide what success is for us with no limits; we do this by writing our own story.

I'm particularly drawn to the origins of *prosper*, from Old Latin terms translating as "according to expectation, according to one's hope," as per the Online Etymology Dictionary.[31] Isn't that what we mean by writing our own story? I seriously doubt you picked up this book hoping to be broke or struggling financially. Prosperity is about money, but it's more than that. Prosperity pertains to our whole life and the ability to live it on our terms, with health, wealth, joy, and belonging. Prosperity is about abundance to live in plenty, not in lack.

I didn't grow up with much money and grew my career to enjoy earning more money than I had ever dreamed. So you can say I've been on both sides of the coin. I grew up in a mobile home on an acre of land on my grandfather's farm outside a very small town in the Midwest. I've also owned a twenty-three-acre estate with two lakes and a custom-built home—and many houses and apartments in between. In a year's time, I've gone from having multiple elaborate vacations to counting change in the car's console to buy my lunch. I've been up, and I've been down.

Here's what I know to be absolutely and unapologetically true about money in life and business: we can't function well in life or do business without it. There you have it. Money is critical, like food, water, shelter, and sleep, so we must discuss it. If you've found a way to thrive without money, please go to any of my social media platforms and message me right now. I must know your secret. If you've figured out how to thrive without money, I'm guessing you're not selling your secret; you're giving it away.

Money is fundamental to life. We need food. We buy it. We need shelter and safety; we buy it. We want a vacation; we buy it. Our business needs money to operate. Our church needs money to function. Our schools need money to educate our youth. Our nonprofit organization needs money to serve.

I'm a colossal Jesus-loving, Bible-reading girl, so I'll just hit this verse head-on, "For the love of money is the root of all evil" (1 Timothy 6:10). I believe this means to love money above all else with no regard for the human element. I agree with this verse; money doesn't come first. I'm talking about honoring money as the fuel for our personal stories. Being poor doesn't make you more holy; it makes you unable to serve in big, bold, human ways. And P.S., Jesus wasn't poor, but I'll let you do your own research on that. This is precisely why I very intentionally put story first and money second.

One of my favorite pastors, Dr. JoLynne Whittaker, writes, "Money by itself is a neutral commodity. The same lump sum can open a homeless shelter or a strip bar. That depends on the heart of the person and who they serve."[32] How you view and use money is a reflection of your story. Write a beautiful story full of love and respect with a high regard for serving humans, connect it to a healthy and functional money-making model, and watch it prosper.

So many words and phrases about money are thrown around willy-nilly from our upbringing, not from a healthy pattern of assurance: *money is power; only assholes have money; I don't care about the money; people where I'm from never have money.* Our mindset about money is often a little jaded, which then churns up our Sea of Uncertainty. Because we are our own first responders, we have the power to change our narrative about money.

First we need to recognize the old patterns so that we can write a new story. The old patterns are the stories we tell ourselves, often passed down from our families.

I work with a lot of high-achieving professional women and the majority have a "poor little girl" money story. Many have become successful to never be that poor little girl again but often are still clinging to some fear that it could all disappear because there's no healthy pattern and narrative in their story center about money. Their money stories sometimes keep them from investing in themselves or believing that even bigger is possible.

A client of mine had arrived at a place of success, affording her a new home and so many things she hadn't had as a child. She earned her way to these things with hard work and discipline. After taking on a CEO role for a tech start-up, our coaching sessions had an unexpected theme; we often discussed her minivan. She wasn't cool enough because she drove a minivan. Would her younger and much hipper colleagues take her seriously because she drove a minivan? It wasn't that she couldn't afford a "cooler ride," and having three children made a minivan a sensible choice. The issue went much deeper.

One day after a session, walking to our cars in the parking lot, she said, "Hey, come look!" Parked in the front row was a Mercedes SUV, and she was beaming. She quickly told me, "It's used, and we got a great deal." It was beautiful, and she was so proud. We high-fived, and I gushed over the new wheels and the great deal. The beautiful ride was fitting of a strong, powerful executive.

Later while discussing money stories in a group session with other high-achieving women, she shared this little nugget, and things made a lot more sense about her minivan angst. The money story passed down in her home was "people with money were assholes." The dinner table discussion often included degrading people with money, even their family members. She vividly remembered, "Well, of course they would act that way with all their money to throw around, what assholes." There you have it, the money story. Of course, she was apprehensive about buying a new vehicle because the first time she pulled into her parents' driveway she would be one of the assholes. She was stuck in the middle of not wanting to be an asshole and wanting to drive a cool vehicle purchased with money she had earned in her role as a successful tech CEO.

Another client, while working on her business strategy, shared the various components of her business. She began jumping from one aspect of the company to another without really executing any of them thoroughly. As I worked with her, it wasn't a matter of not focusing; it was trying to find the next thing to validate her right to be in business. While her husband was a successful doctor and they lived in a beautiful part of town, the fear of poverty they both grew up in kept her chasing after the next big thing. She was afraid of *not accomplishing* as much as she was fearful of *accomplishing*. Who was she to be successful? She was a poverty kid— that was her money story.

Recently a client found the block that had been preventing her from hiring the executive assistant she desperately needed to grow her business. Her money story started in a childhood with meager financial means and parents who worked diligently never to look poor, constantly polishing shoes and showing up clean and neat with whatever they had. She learned that stretching a dollar was valuable and never to look uncomfortable, unkempt, or poor. Just be grateful for what you have. In her business, she was quick to take on projects to keep her team from being burdened. She was taking on work far below her pay grade. Each time we discussed hiring the executive assistant to free her to do more strategic work, she would find a way to channel those funds into other parts of her business. She was accustomed to doing without what she needed to provide for others. *Just polish your shoes and stretch the dollar.*

After digging into this money story, I explained she was robbing the company of growth by not using her gifts and talents to work strategically. The company would grow only to the level she could physically work each week. And with the burnout she was experiencing, she was already stunting the organization's growth unintentionally. Changing this mindset was a breakthrough for her to hire the assistant. She didn't need the assistant because she was irresponsible in managing her time. The organization's growth strategy needed her to work differently. Hiring an assistant would allow her to get more rest, enjoy her life, and delegate with a mindset of growth and abundance.

Just yesterday, a young man told me of a friend who had chosen a simple life with a great company. He was married, living in a modest neighborhood, and his father viewed him as a disappointment because he hadn't decided to pursue a career with more money. His father believes he wasted his life by living modestly—a money story. Deciding to work to achieve wealth isn't good or bad—it's our choice. We're writing our own story.

Think about your personal money story. Quickly write down the first word that comes to mind when you say or hear the word *money*. Spend some time thinking about how you have thought and felt about money. Is it holding you back today? Is your money story based on fear and lack or abundance? How has a money story affected your career choices?

Career Choices

How did you choose the career you are in currently? Typically, careers are chosen based on the five or six careers you were exposed to as a child. We knew of the jobs our parents had, teachers, doctors, what your neighbor or your uncle did, and that's about it. For the hundreds of career women I've worked with, this is their story. They picked a career based on a very narrow perspective of options and someone else's recommendation. These careers were chosen pre-internet when our worlds were small and we had no idea the full scope of options available to us. I rarely come across a client who had anyone spend time asking them what they loved to do, what they were good at, and how they'd like to explore careers using their interests and talents. The primary driver for most career choices was, "Can you make a decent living?"

We were advised to pick careers largely based on our ability to earn a steady paycheck without a lot of discussion first about who we are and how we'd like to spend our days doing this work. Well-meaning loved ones hoped to steer us away from the discomfort of swimming in the Sea of Uncertainty. Then society piled on the belief that college is the most certain path to a steady income and therefore a good life—with no regard for the possibility that college might not be for everyone or that careers working with your hands are fundamental to our society.

Even worse is the narrative to do whatever it takes to earn money your entire adult life, 50 to 66 years, and then you can have meaning at the end of your life. *Pick a career in an industry where you can make money. Don't be concerned about your personal desires and interests. Save those for retirement.*

We use the phrase "Make a living." I would say this is actually called "Earn a paycheck"— money first, then story. If I were to describe making a living, I'd describe it as *write your own story, decide the life you want, how you want to feel in that life, and then design a career to use your talents to make money to fund that life.* Making a living is story plus money.

Too often, college graduates start their adult life with mountains of student loan debt still unsure of their talents, unsure of the life they want to live, and unaware of how to build wealth with their gifts. This is a tough way to get started. The burden of college debt keeps many stuck in careers that do nothing to honor their story and completely stifle their curiosity to explore other career options. This was Amber's story.

Amber radiates. When she walks into a room, the room immediately becomes brighter. And yet she had this "searching" feel about her, like she never felt settled, unsure in what she was supposed to be doing in her career, with her life. As a career mom working in tech sales with five kids and still on the early side of midlife, her days are long just keeping up with the activities of her young kids and the daily quest of "What's for dinner?" Amber's quest to be on the "right path" was palpable.

She was the first in her family to attend college. She had generations of hard-working family members but no college degrees before she earned one. A career in TV broadcasting seemed so fitting for her outgoing personality and desire to connect with people in a meaningful way. The day after 9/11, though, Amber realized she was not built to spread bad news. After spending eighty thousand dollars on her degree, an astronomical amount for her and her family, she felt she had wasted their money. Her search and quest for the "right path" was really about looking for a way to not feel the shame for not using the degree her family had paid for. She felt that if she wasn't a TV newscaster per her original plan, she must be a failure, that she had wasted the money on her education. In her striving mindset, her degree was the pass or fail of external validation. If you spend eighty thousand dollars on something you don't use, you've failed your family. This money story became an eighty-thousand-pound weight she carried around for years. She was constantly looking to validate her worth today and into the future. How could she be worth eighty thousand dollars?

Amber spent time in reflection on her individuality in my seven-month Rise & Thrive Experience. She took notice of how she used her gifts to be valuable and relevant. Her sparkling personality and deep desire to connect with people was impossible not to notice. What she thought would make her a great TV newsperson did in fact make her a great waitress and a mom. When she was offered a job in tech sales, she laughed at the notion of anything tech since she was struggling to use a new cell phone. But she later learned her interest in truly knowing people and connecting with them made her a great salesperson, especially one devoted to solving problems for her clients. She has colleagues who know all of the tech skills, and she's the people connector. She's using the power of her abilities to connect the company to the community, connecting customers to their best solutions. The talents that had attracted her to TV broadcasting are the exact skills she's using to share good news in her company and the community.

Amber has also gone to seminary school while working as an executive and raising a family. She's flipped the script to share the good news, not the bad news! No longer looking to recover from her eighty thousand dollar "wasted degree," her shame has lifted. She knows her purpose is to be a light and a connector, whether with her clients, her kids, and whatever the next chapter of her story brings. She's no longer searching for the picture on the cover of the puzzle box. She's searching for more pieces of the puzzle she can connect. She trusts that when she shows up as herself, she finds the connections she needs and the connections others need from her.

Believing we have to stick with the career we chose as a teenager or else we've failed keeps far too many talented people stuck in shame and striving. Amber learned many things during her college experience that she uses today. The stories she has accumulated and the lessons learned are in her story center to draw from now and well into the future.

What if quitting something we don't love is the path to finding more of what we are made for? What if we don't allow ourselves to explore new things because we see quitting as a failure? What if we were asked to practice lots of things early in life with the sole purpose to find what we loved, experience what we felt great doing? What if we found the things we loved enough to practice and then got really good at them? What if the first thirty or forty years of our life were about exploration before we claimed a "life major"? What if there were guides who came alongside us asking us challenging questions but never expecting us to have the answers just yet? What if our early years were spent learning to study our stories, gifts, and journeys? Sure, we'd work doing this and make money to provide for ourselves, but we wouldn't be pressured to know our career path until we truly knew ourselves.

Lindsay Boccardo is a dear friend, a coach, and a keynote speaker with richly diverse life experiences. She learned about herself so intentionally by trying lots of things as a teenager. She wasn't afraid to start and quit things that weren't interesting to her. She learned what she loved and who she was by paying attention. For example, after trying many instruments, she kept coming back to drums because that was the instrument she loved most to practice. So often we're only looking for what we're good at. Lindsay instead noticed what she liked to spend her time doing.

When choosing a career if you're seventeen or fifty-seven, start with story, reflect on your talents and choose something that aligns. Author Shawn Achor teaches us in his book *The Happiness Advantage* that doing what you love makes you a better performer.[33] When using your gifts and talents in a meaningful way, there's a greater sense of satisfaction in the daily work. You're not just more satisfied; you are actually better at the job. Being better at the job motivates you to do more. Being motivated by the innate sense of doing good work is a different level of engagement than just a earning a paycheck. And studies show that you do in fact make more money doing what you are good at and what you love. Going to work in a job you merely tolerate for the paycheck is striving and, in some cases, only surviving.

CHAPTER 10
Your Money-Making Model

In every job in every company there is a money-making model: the fast-food restaurant you flipped burgers at when you were seventeen, the lemonade stand you set up at age seven. There is a money-making model for the artist selling pieces on the street, the stockbroker on Wall Street, the architect, the doctor, the machinist, the graphic designer, the project manager. Every job is attached to a money-making model. In fact, even someone on public assistance is attached to a money-making model. We don't survive, let alone thrive, without money.

What baffles me is that we don't teach basic business and these money-making models as a core skill as early as middle school. This education is just as important as reading and math. Business is actually a separate college major, but there isn't a career that doesn't rely on a money-making model. Church, school, nonprofits, industry, banking, health care, and service—they all rely on a pretty straightforward money-making formula as the foundation. Money comes in as sales or revenue, money goes out as costs or expenses, and what is left over is reinvested or distributed as profit. This is even true for running your family household.

So why don't we teach business to the masses as a part of our early education? Our education system was modeled in the 1800s after the factory model of business, which was rooted in control. Let's revisit the quote from Seth Godin's manifesto *Stop Stealing Dreams*: "Part of the rationale used to sell this major transformation to industrialists was the idea that educated kids would actually become more compliant and productive workers. Our current system of teaching kids to sit in straight rows and obey instructions isn't a coincidence."[34] The industrialists were not at all interested in prosperity for the masses. They were interested in controlling economics. Why would they put basic business skills into education? Business and money making was *their* job. What's even more troubling to me is we haven't made much, if any, changes to our education system in over a century. Every other aspect of business has seen massive innovation and improvements, but not school. Interesting, isn't it?

Let me be really clear: I'm a fan of people having the freedom to create wealth and distribute it as they see fit. I'm a fan of putting ocean liners of money into the hands of people who will create more companies, more jobs, more opportunities for people to live their personal prosperous stories. I want to live in the Age of Humanity where commerce has the power to heal and create a spark of abundance like we've never seen in our lifetime, not at all like the model we have now. I'm talking about a whole new world. We need a broad, sweeping thriving of the masses; God wired us for it. It's time. It's time for abundance and the understanding of business in the hands and hearts of everyone who goes to work.

And if we're going to create a world of thriving humans through commerce, y'all better get comfortable and educated about money, because a compelling company story isn't enough to sustain that story over time; there must be a sound money-making model. This is where the need to control, measure, and optimize is essential.

Money can be a healthy conversation, like the food groups and sentence structure. Not just personal money management, like how to understand a bank account, but the actual fundamentals of business in early education. Simple things like "Hey, little Johnny, when you take thirty ketchup packets for your fries and only use two and throw the rest away, you just cost that company money."

The first time my kids wanted to set up a lemonade stand, we happily helped them mix their product, and we also explained the cost of the lemonade mix, the rental of our equipment, pitcher, table, and real estate. These were the expenses for their business. Once they sold their product and paid their expenses, then they could enjoy their profits. We looked at marketing techniques, location, and packaging. There is no shame in a healthy money-making model to fund a business that serves its customers with integrity and a compelling story. Money fuels the story. This is how we inspire and empower growth. The more money that flows to the bottom line of a business, family, or person's wealth, the more we fund our options, innovation, and sustainability and the more humans we can serve.

As I work with leaders and ask, "What percentage of your organization can explain the money-making model of your business and how their role contributes to it?" the numbers are abysmal, usually 50 percent or less. I find this fascinating. Companies need money to operate; they seek to make money and grow. And yet, most people within the organization don't know how they fit into the money-making model and how they can help grow the business in their daily choices. Growing the business isn't just the role of the leaders or the sales team; every role has impact on the money-making model. A conscious awareness from every employee about how to grow the business provides an infinite opportunity for growth.

Hear me loud and clear when I say this: It is OUR responsibility to understand the money-making model of the organization. It is OUR responsibility to know how our specific role fits into the money-making model. We're writing our own story and looking for ways to be most valuable and relevant.

You don't need an MBA or a finance degree to know the basics of business. You don't need to be a leader to know the money-making model of your business. Start by drawing a basic version of the money-making model of your company. List all the ways money comes into the organization: sales/revenue, donations, grants, whatever it is for your business. List the way money is spent. What does the company do with the money that is left over? Where does your role fit? This is a start and will likely spark some questions that can lead you to learn more about your company, your industry, and most significantly, your role.

Overly simplistic? Yes and no. This begins your journey to learn more about your company and your industry. When you show up to work you are an expense until you add value and have impact. Your work is expected to have a financial impact. Money is the cornerstone of every organization.

Having a firm grasp on how you affect the organization's money-making model empowers you to offer relevant suggestions for problem-solving and innovation. When you throw an idea out to your boss and it has no value to the money-making model, your manager is left to have the tough conversation and say no to your idea, but not because it wasn't a good idea; it just wasn't relevant to the money-making model. Even worse is the manager who says yes to your idea because they didn't have the courage to say no. Then you put time and effort into something that has no value, so it won't likely get any support and you'll feel frustrated and defeated. When we write our own story, we don't wait for permission; we learn the company story and the money-making model and we confidently go searching for ways to make a difference and grow the business.

As I mentioned earlier, I was blessed to work for an amazing business owner, Don Taylor. Don shared the profit and loss statement with every single employee for each office location. He also taught us how to read and understand the money-making model of the business. I was in my early twenties and hadn't yet obtained my college degree. I had run away from home at 18 and sought other adventures in bartending, waitressing, managing the office work for my grandfather's plumbing business, and other fascinating roles. I learned more from Don than any of my college classes I later paid for.

Don taught us how the business worked in simple terms. I knew how my role affected the sales and the bottom-line profit of the business. When I made good placements—meaning I hired the right people for our clients and they stayed for the entire assignment or went on to be hired by the client—we made far more money. If I made a poor placement and had to replace that person several times until I got it right, that took more time and money, causing less money to go to the bottom line.

This was important because Don shared a percentage of the profits with every single employee. Our receptionist knew the money-making model. She was also in charge of ordering our office supplies. Once she figured out that spending more money on office supplies meant money out of her pocket, she got serious. You had to be ready to justify your use of too many sticky notes because she wasn't messing around. She cared about the bottom line of the company, and she shared in it.

We kept whiteboards in our office to track our work and progress. We knew every single day how many openings for jobs we had and how many we had placed that week. I kept my whiteboard up to date; that was my responsibility. I kept score of my work in the money-making model. I didn't wait for a performance review to know if I was doing a good job or if I was valuable. I knew every day and I knew how to make adjustments daily, not every six months, if I wanted to improve.

We had a new manager for our office. She had management experience and she also had an interior design background. Excited to use her experience in interior design, she set out to redecorate our office. While I am aware that an office environment is important to the brand and the customer experience, I was not excited that she was spending my money to buy new wallpaper. She brought the big wallpaper book into my office, plopped it down on my desk, and asked me to pick out the wallpaper I wanted for my private office. I told her I wouldn't be choosing wallpaper because I didn't approve of spending my portion of the bonus on the wallpaper. Y'all, I was just barely old enough to order my own beer, and I was sassy about someone spending my money!

After a couple of difficult discussions, she sent me to meet with Don. It felt just as uncomfortable as being sent to the principal's office. I didn't fear being fired. Partly because I was young and naive, but I also knew my worth in the company. I was confident in my decision.

After Don took the time to hear me out and listen to my logic, he smiled and leaned over the desk and said, "I don't disagree with you, Rebecca. I absolutely appreciate how seriously you take the bottom line of our company." OUR company. He knew I was invested, and this made him more money too! But, he said, "Our office needs a refresh. I've asked your manager to do this project. Could you please pick out some wallpaper?" I was seen, heard, and understood, and without further argument, I picked out some dusty blue and mauve wallpaper for our office (because it was the '80s).

Don honored the manager's story first, then money, but it's the power of knowing both that enables us to thrive in business. I'm sure he had promised the manager the redecorating project as a part of her employment. I can now see that her skills as a designer were of significant value to the company, as we were expanding and opening new offices quickly.

There is great personal power in knowing the money-making model of your business. While I worked for a large training and development company, a leader once said about me to a group of colleagues, "Rebecca doesn't really need a manager." At the time, I was a sales executive working on the front lines. I didn't hold a leadership title; I held a leadership mindset. On the organizational chart, of course I reported to a manager. I was several levels from the top. What he meant by the comment was that I made it my job to understand how the company operated. I didn't wait to be told what to do or understand how the company worked; I made it my responsibility to know how to help the company grow. I asked questions to understand the pay structure of the consultants I placed to do work with my clients. I learned how in some cases if I charged just $100 more for an engagement, a consultant could earn $500 more in their own pocket. I honored my colleagues' stories as well as the company story. I learned the margins of our products and how to create solutions that were first highly impactful to our clients and then highly profitable to our company. Story first, then money. This works only if you know both. I wasn't afraid to ask questions and sometimes to challenge appropriately. In many cases I knew more than my manager about the money-making model of our company.

I went on to get my degree in business management while holding a job with a six-figure paycheck as an executive for the staffing company that Don later sold and retired from. My degree was validation. I had already paid the price to learn and understand business while doing the work. Honestly, other than the perceptions and stereotypes I faced about not having a degree, especially as a consultant, it didn't help me at all in my career.

You don't need a Harvard degree or a degree at all to learn the money-making model of a business. Start with basics and build based on your industry. I wish I had the money back I invested in that degree. I would have received a much higher return on the investment of those dollars had I invested that money into my current business.

Money comes into the organization as sales, revenue, donations—these are assets; money is spent, and these are expenses; what is left over is profit to be distributed or reinvested. No need to overcomplicate this.

Basic Business for Humans:

1. You start out as an expense for the business. This doesn't mean you don't have personal worth. Your personal worth comes from your uniqueness. It's up to you to use your gifts to add value to the organization.

2. Once you add value above what you are paid in salary and benefits, then you begin to be an asset. Your salary will always

show up on the company profit and loss statement as an expense. The value you provide to the money-making model in doing your work shows up as an asset.

3. Your value does not come from your title; it comes from the impact you have to the company story and the money-making model.

4. The more you know yourself and intentionally add value to the company story and the money-making model, the more relevant you are to the company.

5. The more relevant you are to the company, the more autonomous and confident you are, and the more courageous you are to innovate and increase your value.

6. Waiting to be "developed" lets someone else write your story.

Navigating the Money-Making Model

The money provides fuel for the story. The money-making model is created through strategy, goals, metrics, systems, and processes. Think of these as the transportation system of your business. Why does a transportation system exist? To get you where you want to go safely and swiftly. We don't build roads for the sake of roads; we build roads to help humans get where we want to go. Our money-making model should follow the same intent and help humans navigate and grow the organization safely and swiftly. Think of safety as psychologically safe, creating assurance and confidence versus uncertainty.

Let's break this down. You are writing your personal story each day by reflecting on and understanding who you are, what makes you unique, what gifts you have to offer. Let's say your personal story goes shopping for a vehicle to get you where you want to go. The vehicle is your role in a company story. This is also the vehicle you will drive your gifts around in to serve others. Like taking a driver's exam, you've prepared to drive any vehicle by knowing yourself well. You then choose a vehicle, aka a job or career that fits your current needs. It's likely your first vehicle wasn't a semitruck or a private plane; it was a reasonable car you could afford and felt safe driving. You learned to drive and maybe had a few fender benders in that first vehicle. That's how we learn. Over time we upgrade our vehicles to fit our needs and lifestyle, much like we upgrade our roles and careers as we learn more about ourselves, add value, and get promoted.

You are responsible for your vehicle, your career. You keep your car well maintained, you put fuel in the vehicle and take it through the car wash once in a while. This is your vehicle, your career. You then learn to navigate the company story with your vehicle. You learn the rules of the road and where you're going.

Next we head out onto the road, the money-making model. In a company, how we navigate and transport the work from one place to the next is the strategy, the goals, the systems, and the processes. We need roads that are well maintained, lighted, and have great signage.

Not everyone is responsible for building the transportation system, but we are responsible for knowing how to navigate it. We download maps, we read the signs, and we keep our vehicle in good working order so we don't break down and create a road hazard. Sometimes we get flat tires and someone comes along to help us. But it is our responsibility to know the road system we are on just as it is our responsibility to know the money-making model of the organization. What is the strategy, where is it taking us, how will I know if I'm on the right road, where do I go for routine maintenance, whom am I traveling with, are we all driving on the correct side of the road, are we late or on time?

Company leaders in this metaphor are the engineers, responsible for mapping out the transportation system for our work, designing the roads and bridges. Some leaders are responsible for knowing when it's time to upgrade from a gravel road to a paved one. Some fill potholes. As an employee, you are responsible to report large potholes, stalled vehicles, or poor signage. You may be a leader responsible for creating better lighting on the signs or reporting a temporary roadblock or a detour.

The company story tells who we are on the roads and where we're going together. The money-making model is the transportation system that helps everyone work together to get where we're going safely and swiftly with some road trip snacks and stops for fuel and to see some scenery along the way.

The leader's role is ensuring the money-making model serves as a simple roadway system to transport the work from employee to employee and then to the customers and showing the employees how the roadway system works. Leaders ensure the roads of the money-making model don't slow down the work, like too many unnecessary approvals or no context as to why the systems matter.

Too often, especially in large organizations, the systems become like a complicated freeway system that intimidates some drivers and brings rage to others. In a small startup organization, people learn to navigate rough terrain with pure grit and stamina to get where they want to go, like off-roading in a truck looking for the best route. Some entrepreneurs need a better roadway system but they like the adrenaline of off-roading, so they frustrate the other drivers trying to work with them. To fuel the growth of an organization's money-making model, strategies, goals, systems, and processes should be simple, well lit, well maintained, and with easy-to-read signs and guardrails in place for the difficult twists and turns. Sometimes the best thing you can do to increase the growth of your company is build a clear and concise transportation system for the money-making model. Leaders, take some time to review the money-making model for your role. Do you need better lighted signs, a few potholes fixed, or maybe that gravel road paved? Employees, could you be helpful by kindly reporting potholes or traffic jams?

An easy-to-understand example of the money-making model is a company sales forecast with each person understanding their role and the need to meet their sales quota. This is how leaders plan resources for the company. Clear and reasonable goals keep us stretching and growing. I'm happy to work to achieve sales goals, and it's my job to know and honor that system.

At times sales leaders would come to me and say, "Hey, if you bring in a little extra revenue this quarter, we'll throw you more money, a trip, or a prize." *SPIFFs*, they're called, sales performance incentives. Guess what? I hated this. It was as if they'd said, *You probably could have served your clients more this month, Rebecca. Could you go out and do more of that? Then I'll pat you on the head and give you an extra treat.* At one point I called my leader and said, "I need you to stop letting people call me with these offers." I seriously wanted to quit. I was in the top percentile of the company as a sales contributor. I was no slacker. I knew my goals, and I exceeded them.

You can understand the leader's motive. Give an incentive to the good ones because they know how to do it. Not so ironically, once I had met my sales quotas I would often contact my colleagues to see how I could help them. This did not win me more money or trips; it fed my desire to serve other humans.

My deepest desire is to be valuable and relevant to serve my clients, to solve their problems, and to help them achieve their goals. The human-to-human work brings out the best version of ourselves. I was paid well for my talents because my human-to-human desire to connect and serve enabled me to meet my sales goals year over year. The requests for me to bring in more money without the connection to the human story made me feel like a machine.

Reward me for the value I bring to the client and the appreciation for hitting my goals, and then let me rest. Pushing top performers year over year in ways that move them further from the human-to-human connection and more about a number on a spreadsheet is a path to burnout. I'm not a machine; I'm not here to produce and get my pat on the head, big paycheck, and glass award. I'm here to make a difference. I'm here to connect with other humans, to form teams, and to serve the humans in business.

To continue the transportation system metaphor, if a company isn't hitting sales targets early in the quarter, you assess the vehicles the employees have on the road. Do some need routine maintenance? Do some need to find other vehicles? Are the signs well lit, or are some people lost? Are the roads clear and well maintained? A company helps everyone get to the destination and doesn't run its top performers far past their limits. Instead, fuel the top performers up with a healthy paycheck and maybe a car wash and a tune-up while the drivers take a break. You wouldn't put a race car out on the track with an exhausted driver. There's a reason airlines have a required rest and sleep schedule for their pilots.

When I look back over my career in sales, as I shifted my focus and put a higher priority on meeting the sales goal over serving the customer and their human needs, the lower my satisfaction fell in the job. The less valuable and relevant I felt and the less engagement I felt to my company. We all have an innate desire to serve another human which is greater than our desire to hit a number or a goal with no human context. The more my personal brand story shifted to numbers on a spreadsheet and less about my story of serving clients, the more tired I became and less motivated to go above and beyond. The more I stretched to reach higher and higher sales quotas, the more disconnected I felt from my clients and from my personal story, like being trapped on a roundabout or freeway loop without really going anywhere.

This happens even in great companies. This is an unintended consequence. It's also an important lesson for leaders: never lose sight of the human story of your employees and customers and how they connect. Story first, then money; it is our responsibility as leaders to know both. Build a money-making model to transport the story, communicate with clarity and context why the goals, systems, and processes matter to the humans. The great news, starting with story then combining with money, makes for a life with more meaning and more money, purpose, and profit.

How are you doing connecting story and money? Here's a little road map for you to assess where you might be and what you might do to move closer to thriving.

Personal Story	Company Story	Money-Making Model	Survive, Strive, or Thrive?	Description
Employees know their unique skills and how to use them in their role.	Employees know the mission, vision, and culture and the why and the how for the customer and the company.	Employees know how the company makes money, the value they provide to the customer in relation to the money-making model, and how their role contributes to it.		
Y	Y	Y	Thrive	Powerful, engaged, innovative, autonomous, profitable, growth oriented. They know who they are, the company story, the money-making model, and how to grow the company.
Y	Y	N	Strive	Evangelist, committed. They can be dangerous because their ideas and voice are compelling but not necessarily intentional or profitable. Their strong voice can lead people in ways that aren't affecting the bottom line and sustainability of the organization.
Y	N	Y	Strive	In it for themselves, anxious for rewards and SPIFFs, great for short-term growth, quarter-end sprints. They are dangerous because they could sacrifice the customer or the company integrity for personal gain.
Y	N	N	Strive	Likely to manipulate the system for personal gain, no loyalty. They could be climbing the corporate ladder to win at all cost, with no regard for the culture, the customer, or the bottom line.

Continued on next page

Continued

Personal Story	Company Story	Money-Making Model	Survive, Strive, or Thrive?	Description
N	Y	Y	Strive	Will change and adapt for the company with no regard for their personal needs. They likely suffer burnout serving the company, which is followed by bitterness and resentment.
N	Y	N	Strive	The martyr tirelessly represents the people within the organization with no regard to their own needs or the financial growth and sustainability of the organization.
N	N	Y	Strive	The first to lead a private equity firm. Turnaround agent. They get what they can out of their role or the company and move on, whatever it takes, with no regard for personal or company story, impact, or consequences.
N	N	N	Survive	They come for a paycheck only, are tough to manage, will leave for a quarter more across the street. They resist change and aren't interested in learning anything new, improving, or thinking critically. Let them go.

PART III
Rhythm

CHAPTER 11
Letting Go of Control: Flow, Not Force

The key of rhythm unlocks the third door to a life of flourishing, a much more human life than simply being productive: a life honoring the emotional flow of our human story first versus the control dictated by the factory. Life already consists of rhythm. God-given rhythms persist in nature, music, speech, art, breath, and our pulse. To thrive, choose to step into natural rhythms. Honor your emotions and the uncertainty of living and working with other humans. Unlike striving to control, rhythm is connection, open minds, open hearts, open hands.

Like the ebb and flow of the tides, the change of the seasons, the rising and setting of the sun, there is a natural flow in how we were created to live in harmony with the world around us. Rhythm lets things come and go, grow and evolve, give and receive. Rhythm is connection over control.

When all these factors are judiciously treated by the performer with regularity yet with artistic purpose, there is an effect of forward movement and not mere machine-like accuracy, to paraphrase Encyclopedia.com.[35] This description of rhythm really got to me:

rhythm covers the grouping of notes into beats, beats into measures, and measures into phrases.

We are human. We are the performing artist, not a machine. We bring our story to life and do our work with artistic purpose. Our lives are meant to be lived, loved, and embraced. We bring the highs and lows of our emotions, the joys and struggles—all the elements of an epic story. Rhythm asks us how we feel, not just what we've accomplished. Life is so much more than our inbox and a promotion. The combination of our human needs and business needs meet in rhythm and cadence, creating forward movement. We're built for rhythm, not machine-like repetition without feeling. We're more like houseplants than machines. We need food, water, and sunlight to thrive, and we grow better with great humans around us that talk nicely to us. We want and need to flourish, not just be productive.

Rhythm honors the emotional flow of our lives, the highs and lows of our personal story. Rhythm connects story and money to create the Age of Humanity by honoring our human needs first and using our personal story to give commerce a social construct. Rhythm wants value, relevance, and impact, not punching a time clock.

Like music, our lives are meant to be felt and to move us. What's the difference between listening to a song or an alarm clock? The steady beat of an alarm clock—you immediately want to shut it down, it's annoying, and your brain can't take it! Living a life of productivity feels like the alarm clock blaring, controlled, consistent, unwavering. *Beep, beep, beep.* The first thing we think is "Make it stop!" It's too consistent, too controlled; our brains receive it as an attack because it's not natural. This is the sound of controlled striving.

A song is so very different, the highs and lows of varied melody and rhythm draw us in emotionally to engage with the music. Rhythm has uncertainty, surprise, pause, and crescendo. Write and honor your story with the beautiful rhythm of a song that draws you in and engages you emotionally, letting the emotions and the messiness flow.

Take out a piece of paper, position it "landscape," and grab a pen. On the far left of the page write your date of birth. On the far right of the page write today's date. Draw a line to connect those two dates, the timeline of your life. Now think through the years moving up and down based on the highs and lows of your life all the way to today. There could be the lows of childhood trauma, the highs of overcoming and landing a great job, the lows of losing a parent, the highs of beautiful children, the lows of being fired. You get the idea. Does it look like a waveform? Think of a visual of a voice recording: a waveform visually represents rhythm and sound. When portrayed in color it is also a "heat map" showing intensity through color, like when sound "pegs in the red." This is your life, the highs and lows, brightness and dullness, good times and struggles.

Living our story in rhythm means we expect the ups and downs as a natural part of life. We learn from the struggles in ways that dramatically shape us and our story. Our story matters, including the struggle. Look back at the highs and lows of your timeline and ask yourself what you've learned in each of those low points. We derive strength and resilience from our struggles. By seeing our life as a story, we take comfort in knowing our struggles can be just a chapter of our lives, not our entire lives. We have the ability to reflect, connect, and initiate changes in our lives.

In the early days of my divorce, I sat in reflection preparing for the days ahead. I thought to myself, *Okay, this is going to suck, probably worse than you can imagine. And if you can find a way to remain upright and empathic throughout the process, you can come out of this better, not bitter. Give yourself two to three years to get on the other side.* I set my intention for who I was going to be as I navigated these challenging times. I was creating the conditions to thrive inside the struggle.

Each night I would check in with myself. How had I navigated that day? What did I learn about myself, and how could I use it to help me be better tomorrow? Each night I reminded myself I was one day closer to being on the other side of a really sucky chapter. Even though

I wasn't sure what the future would hold, I knew I was progressing. I also knew I had very little control over anything but my mindset and my choices. I released everything into a rhythm of ebb and flow, come and go, highs and lows.

Letting Go of Control

We're looking for flow, not force. First we have to open our minds, our hearts, then our hands to let go of some control. I've got some troubling news: we are not in control of the universe, and we're never getting caught up. I know, I know. This is tough to hear. Take a few moments and breathe deeply. You're going to be okay. Instead embrace the reality that life is messy and uncertain. And sometimes it's a beautiful mess because uncertainty is the demonstration of growth. If your life doesn't have the discomfort of uncertainty, you're not growing. If you're not growing, you're dwindling and wilting.

We've actually been prepped for this uncertainty. The Bible states 365 times "fear not." God knew we'd be dealing with messy and uncertain as a part of our human experience, so He equipped us with a daily dose of "I got you." Unfortunately, we're so busy running around trying to do "all the things," we forget we're not in control and somehow responsible for everything and everyone.

When we continually rush ahead to fix everything we don't leave room for God as our Creator to be the orchestrator. We don't acknowledge the learning from the messes or allow the supernatural and divine happenings that make us better and take as farther along than we could have planned for ourselves. You know those times, when the person who sits next to us in a coffee shop is the answer to our latest problem or when the perfect client for our business casually walks through the door. And sometimes when a relationship leaves our life unexpectedly, rather than chase it down to fix it and save it, maybe we should let it go. We could rest far more if we let God do His thing and stayed the heck out of the way, letting the rhythm of things come and go like an ocean tide.

With our desire to control and achieve, there's little room left for the supernatural work for God to be God. I shudder to think the number of times I've blocked a blessing or a divine connection because I was determined to get ahead of the situation rather than let things play out. Or how often I could have rested my tired, busy brain and relinquished my own control to the calming effect of prayer rather than another late night looking at reports and details trying to anticipate and solve the next challenge for me, my family, or my team.

Sometimes I picture God on this huge asphalt paving truck trying to lay the road before me to give me a smooth ride. I'm running up ahead slowing Him down, tapping Him on the shoulder, asking when the road will be done, wondering why He is going this way, and what about this and what about that. In my vision, He takes a big deep sigh and says, "Why don't you go over there and rest and let me do my work. We'll all benefit from you getting out of the way more often and getting more sleep."

When we try to live a machine-like life of control, we strive and battle against natural rhythms. I won't go into a deep dive of circadian rhythms; however, a brief story from nature will give context. In the morning hours, many flowering plants unfold their leaves and petals to the light and fold them back up at night. In the 1700s, French scientist Jean-Jacques d'Ortous de Mairan wondered what would happen if he put mimosa plants in complete darkness, you know, controlling things as we humans like to do. Surprisingly, the mimosa plants continued to open and close from their internal clocks, not from the impact of the light. They weren't responding to the light; they were expecting it.[36] Our natural rhythms are a part of being a living creature. We can't stop those natural rhythms even when we try to control or fight against them.

Like the mimosa plants, we also have internal clocks, built-in rhythms. In 1990, biologist Michael Rosbash discovered normal fruit flies also possessed this twenty-four-hour cycle of light and dark as do we humans.[37] Again, circadian rhythms. Our biological makeup is beautiful, fascinating, and a part of nature. We are not in control of the "light"; we are here to expect it and live in rhythm with it. Our obsession with control happened when we moved from living in concert with nature, the changing weather, and abounding faith in the "light" of the agrarian society to the control of time in the factory. Even adding artificial light was a significant change to how we value our natural rhythms. While we enjoy the convenience of flipping on a light switch in the kitchen at 9 p.m., it's steered our attention away from the natural light and rhythms of nature and our human needs.

Clock In, Clock Out: The Great Time Fallacy

The industrial age taught us to value all things time bound. This obsession with time leads to an obsession of getting more done and doing it quickly versus asking ourselves what we feel, what we need, and then doing the right things for us, looking for opportunities to pare back to create space for opportunity and rest. Our obsession with time doesn't honor the rhythm of living and working in flow; it says "more" and "hurry." *More* and *hurry* rarely work out like we think they should. *More* should be for human things like love, mercy, grace, and listening.

Undoing our obsession with time, more, and hurry means that quitting isn't failure. Resting isn't failure. Pausing isn't failure. These are a part of the rhythm, a part of your human needs. In a world that has honored more, faster, and hurry, learning to stop and rest takes great intention. I recently worked with a client who is doing valuable work, being paid well, and doing it in a way so that she has ample time to coach her daughter's soccer team and not work at night or on the weekends. She loves her life and at the same time wonders if she's not challenging herself enough or doing it "right" because she's not as stressed and overwhelmed as her peers.

In the Age of Humanity, we see rest, quitting, and pause as a part of the work, not what we do when we're not working. When we stop doing, we create space. Our time available each day is finite. I know you're a badass, I know you can accomplish more than most, but at some point, you have to ask yourself, at what expense? Using our time for rest and recovery or quitting something to create space, rejuvenates our focus and our ability to flourish.

Workwise, the trend in the last ten years is to book shorter and shorter meetings—believing there will be more time left in the day to achieve more and get more done—when, in fact, it's just created more meetings on the calendar. The reason for the meeting and the time necessary to solve the problem aren't taken into consideration. No clarity, no intent, no context, no thoughtful pondering about how much discussion and interaction is necessary for the topics at hand, just a block of time.

We book meetings conducive to the eight-hour workday versus asking ourselves, "What am I trying to accomplish? How much time should I allow?" We shoot off quick emails working toward the counterfeit success of inbox zero instead of exploring real solutions with clarity and context. Sometimes we don't even know what problem we're solving; we're just mindlessly responding.

We've all seen the leader who rushes into one meeting ten minutes late, looking and sounding disheveled and distracted, and later, with the meeting barely touching on the big topics that need to be discussed or solved, they jump up, apologizing that they can't stay because they must get to the next meeting. They ask to schedule a follow-up meeting to finish the discussion and create a plan. Everyone knows it could be two to three weeks before the next meeting will get on everyone's calendar.

In truth, this issue could have been explored with rich dialogue, sharing of concerns, and presenting of ideas, then solved with one targeted and intentional three-hour block of time. Yet, in today's world of work, asking for three hours for a meeting is just not the way things are done. We'd rather spend six hours over the next twelve months talking about the issue. Dilbert surely has a cartoon of this. Laughable if it weren't true. The results of control versus connection.

Instead of robotically moving through the schedule in time-bound increments, what if there was great consideration taken on what was to be accomplished, the emotions and concerns of the people involved, and the appropriate amount of time assigned to rich discussion, planning, and problem-solving? Humans need to be seen and heard and to allow conversation and connection to engage in a common approach to move forward.

Instead, many have this striving life of battling time versus seeking connection and impact. I know I did: Get up at 4:30 a.m., bootcamp workout at the gym by 5 p.m., shower and get on the road by seven o'clock, first meeting at 8:15 a.m. Shit, I hope there's no traffic. I'll grab a coffee on the way. Morning meetings ran over, the boss needed another report, no time for lunch, I'll eat a protein bar while on Zoom. Afternoon presentation needs the slides redone. Grab someone from marketing on the way to the retirement party for Joe at three; they can redo the slides in time for me to present at four. What am I presenting again? Oh yeah, new product updates. Wrap the presentation at five o'clock, praying for no real questions that could make me late for daycare pickup by six. Dollar-a-minute late fees are killing me. Pick up the girl, order a pizza on the way to be delivered, too damn tired to cook. Pour wine, eat pizza, bath time for the girl and a quick story. Back to the laptop by 9 p.m.—what's on the schedule for tomorrow?

This is the factory of our lives, more dystopian than utopian. I say this with no shame or guilt; I say this with love, knowing, and sadness because this was my life too. I say this with a lump in my throat, a stress memory response. Sitting at the stoplight, heart pounding, looking at my phone calculating the minutes, could I get there in time? Cortisol pumping through my body, I had nearly perfected the hustle and grind, abetted by a healthy dose of "suck it up, find joy, no worries, you got this" kind of life. I was living a life of endurance, constantly looking to control time. I wasn't honoring any of the conditions for thriving that my brain desperately wanted for me. No nourishing, no stillness, no intentionally working to serve other humans. Just tasks, appointments, and blocks of time with little clarity or context on why any of this shit mattered to others and no understanding of how any of it helped me live the life I wanted. I didn't have time to think about what I wanted.

In fact, controlling time has become the mark of high character. The more one can control time, the better the human they are. (Someone please assign a universal sarcasm font.) Because of this desire to control time and the heroic nature we have placed on the overwhelmed, we now believe:

- organized and punctual = smarter and respectful
- messy and late = lazy and disrespectful

Nope. It's not true. Those desks at school in their neat rows with the same amount of time allocated for each class and the rules about late work not counting for your grade led us to believe if you're not neat and on time, you're not smart or as valuable and relevant. More bullshit. Brilliant people are being left out of important conversations about strategy and solving critical issues and passed over for promotions because they don't return emails promptly or are late for meetings. We place timeliness of a person in the same category as respect and intelligence. Ask yourself, is the person's lateness negatively affecting you? Or are you just annoyed believing your way is the right way. What would extending some grace do for that person? If I'm meeting with someone and they text me frantically, "I'm sorry I'm late!" The kind of message where you can feel their stress. I love responding with "Breathe, be safe, things happen, I'm enjoying a few minutes to relax, I'll see you when you get here."

People who are chronically late are more optimistic, think more quickly on their feet, often have higher intelligence, are interested in many things, and due to their optimism actually may live longer.[38] And yet, because of our addiction to control and order, we look down upon those who can't get to the meeting on time or don't respond to emails by the end of the day. We've adopted time as a social virtue, when in fact, time perception and attention are largely psychological, not based on our character.[39]

I worked with a guy whose mind was brilliant and full of amazing information and experience. Quick on his feet, with tons of stories and metaphors to help clients understand complex problems, he was one of the best consultants I've ever known. Leave him with a group of leaders, a whiteboard, and tough problems to solve and he was a happy camper and an invaluable resource. He's brilliant in a room with clients, human to human. The biggest complaint about working with this guy was his inability to return emails on time and manage his calendar. There was an air of frustration pointed at his care for the job, his ego, and his character. None of these were true. The value he provided in the room with clients far exceeded any of his peers in this role, but his "inefficiencies with time" were perceived as inhibiting his career and his ability to have profound impact.

It was maddening to me why he wasn't assigned administrative support to elevate his strengths and reduce the friction and frustration about time and schedules. A simple puzzle piece solution. You can hear the responses, right? "Well, if we gave him admin support, we'd have to do it for everyone in his role." (Insert an eye roll here so hard it may cause an aneurysm.) No, you don't have to treat everyone the same because we're not all the same. The belief we're all to be treated equal may make your job easier, but we're not all the same. School taught us to value marbles, not puzzles. Everyone, round out your edges and be the same. Be on time and leave class when the bell rings, not when you're done learning or done solving the problem. This is the shift the Age of Humanity will require from leaders. It will take intentional effort, expectation setting, lots of human connection.

For humans like my son with attention deficit disorder, the value of time and organization as a social virtue and marker of future success is a tough pill to swallow. There's so much shame and damage to self-esteem when time and organization are valued above other talents and contribution. In an email exchange with my son's fifth-grade teacher,

I asked about her classroom structure, trying to learn how to support him because he was struggling. She was aware of his attention deficit disorder but had no idea what it actually meant. Her response to my email was, "Cameron needs to be more organized." I was at my wits' end trying to work with her, so I responded, "And the deaf kid needs to listen more, but that's not going to happen, is it?" The following year we moved him into a Montessori school, which was a much better fit for his brain, honored him as an individual, allowing an ebb and flow of rhythm and choice, not the time-bound control of a factory education.

The next time you become frustrated with someone for time management challenges, ask yourself what they bring to the team. Unclench your fist of control and time-bound addictions and open your hands to connect. After writing about the nuances and challenges of attention deficit disorder, a peer in my company reached out to me and said while she previously had been so frustrated by one of our colleagues and his rambling and lack of control, she now realized the immense value he brought to the team.

Rather than looking for ways to get more squeezed into the calendar, what if you looked for ways to do less *better*? What if you decided what was more important to the company story and the money-making model and let some other stuff go? What if you lived connection versus control? Thriving isn't measured by time; it's felt through impact, value, and relevance.

CHAPTER 12
"Caught Up" Isn't a Place

Once upon a time, there were three young girls. They grew up inseparable, laughing and supporting one another through their youth. One grew up to be a wife and a mother, the other went on to a rewarding career in the city, and the third lived with and cared for her grandmother. The girls would connect to chat and catch up every couple of weeks. They'd tell tales of the chaos in their lives. The mom would tell of the kids getting into everything and the constant piles of laundry and exhaustion, the single career girl would talk of the incessant meetings, emails, and the crazy boss she dealt with each week. The girl caring for her grandmother would talk of the endless doctor appointments, trips to the pharmacy, and fights with the insurance company over what bills would be paid. During each phone chat the girls would long to see each other and talk of the day they could meet somewhere for the weekend to share some laughs and connect. And each time, at least one would say, "That sounds great. When I get caught up, let's get together."

And lo and behold there came a day when the mom had all the laundry done and the dishes put away; the kids were clean, fed, and happy; and the husband was happily whistling while he worked. The single career girl had the very same day that her inbox was empty, her boss was grinning, and her clients were paying her well and demanding very little of her time. The girl working and caring for her grandmother had a week off with no doctor appointments, the bills were paid, and papers filed. Grandmother had gone for the week to play bingo with her friends upstate. They quickly booked a trip and met in a wonderful place and laughed and joked and spent the weekend like the girls they had always been. The end.

Can you imagine this happening?

No, because "caught up" is a fairytale myth. It's not a place we "get to." You're NEVER getting caught up. Ever.

"When I get caught up" is the master phrase of striving, battle, and control. "When I get caught up" can be the excuse for staying stuck. And maybe most concerning, the striving attempt to be caught up is how we unintentionally isolate ourselves by trading meaningful connection for controlling and producing. Email is always coming in, there will always be laundry to wash, and there's always another meeting to plan and a soccer game to attend. There is no magical place of bliss and organization called "caught up."

I attempted it for years. I was the queen of hustle. I would put the kids to bed and stay up until early morning responding to emails, always trying for that illusive inbox-zero achievement award. Late into the night, I'd read through pages of my planner, making sure I had sent and done everything I said I would do, then add a few extra tasks for good measure—you know, to "prove myself." Check, check, check.

Whew.

Caught up.

Winning.

Killing the game.

You know what? I would wake up the next day feeling pretty cranky, with responses to some of those emails already waiting on me. The entire day I'd be sluggish. By evening I'd be snapping at the kids for chewing too loud or being indignant. I should have waved the white flag and a sign that read, "It's not you; it's me." But I didn't. Instead, I thought: *Hustle is my job! I'm to be revered and respected for my hustle game! I'm bringing home the bacon and angrily frying it up in a pan while I bitch and moan about stupid stuff that rarely matters because I'm so damn tired from arriving at inbox zero.*

The quest to control time and get caught up consumed much of my thinking. As burnout rolled in, slowly taking more of my breath and quietly drowning me, I was forced to look at this elusive "caught up" prize I was chasing. I did a time study and wrote down all of the things I wanted to accomplish in a week for home and work. I included everything I could think of, from prayers to laundry and the mandatory work meetings in between. I estimated a realistic time associated with each and the average amount of sleep I wanted to get each night, which was less than eight hours. Y'all, I made a spreadsheet for this. Like a dog with a bone, I was going to figure this out. There, in the auto sum box on my spreadsheet, was the hardcore reality that this was actually an unwinnable game. I just stared at the box on the spreadsheet and slowly blinked for a while.

Like my children's baby pictures and my high school yearbook, I wish I had kept that spreadsheet. It became a relic of a life event that changed me in significant ways. This was bullshit. I'm not interested in playing a game I can't win. Milli Vanilli played in a loop in the background, "Girl, You Know It's True." But the lie was exposed. I was living a damn lie!

Here I was evangelizing productivity and the value of living a more balanced life and believing every word of what I taught. To be fair, I helped a lot of people and am grateful for that time. As I thought about my colleagues, the great men I worked alongside, I realized they had wives and "stay at home moms" dividing the labor on that spreadsheet! I was one human trying to do the work of two or more. I was *never getting caught up!* EVER! I started thinking back over my life. Had I ever been caught up? I scanned the past weeks, then months, and went back years. Finally, there it was ... 1987.

I hadn't been caught up since 1987. It was twelve glorious hours I remember like it was yesterday. I was moving back home to Indiana from Florida. Two years prior I had run away from home and spent a couple of years bartending and waitressing in Daytona Beach. I decided it was time to come home. So I packed my car with everything I could fit, leaving the rest behind. For twelve hours I didn't have a job, a house, or any responsibilities other than getting myself back to Indiana. I rolled down the windows, smoked cigarettes, and blasted Ratt and Poison cassette tapes with joy and reckless abandon. There it was, the last time I was ever caught up. For those of you who took the more traditional route and went straight from high school to college, you may have *never* experienced being caught up. It was a magical place, for twelve full hours. Of course, I had to run away from home and school to get there.

Did this mean I had to give up my job and my family to get caught up again? That seemed harsh. What it meant was that I needed a better measure of well-being and success. I needed to let go of the attempt to control all the things in my life. I needed a healthy view of the natural ebb and flow of love and life, work and rest. There was no magical space and place with the laundry done, the inbox zero, the goals met, and the family happy. "Caught up" was a lie I needed to let go. Letting this lie go and writing a new narrative to believe was and always is the first step. I began to reflect on writing a new story. To thrive is to grow. Growth requires evolution and change, bringing something new on and letting something else die away. It's impossible to grow and to control every outcome.

Another aspect of this magical trip returning home was that it was full of uninterrupted thinking and dreaming. The long drive full of anticipation and excitement about the next chapter, being with friends and family and my dreams for the future. Thinking, dreaming, and anticipating is integral to thriving and the natural rhythm of our lives. The opportunity to write in new chapters of our story and to live in '80s-rock-band joy with anticipation of what's coming next. Exploring the story of our lives, not in constant control. We can't put off dreaming until the day when we're caught up. We dream to write a new chapter. What did a thriving life look and feel like in this new chapter I was writing? I wasn't sure I knew. It turns out this is true for many of us high achievers.

I asked a group of two hundred professionals to describe a great and rewarding life as a career professional, the opposite of burnout. As I read the responses, the first challenge appeared. We can effortlessly talk about what we don't want, but we struggle to describe what we do want. We grapple with articulating a great life as a professional. If we're going to craft a plan, we have to know what we're going after. We have to name it to claim it. We can't live the life we want until we can speak the life we want. Complaining and criticizing ourselves in frustration isn't going to get us there. Typed into the margins on the survey, comments read: "This is hard!" and "I've never really thought about it." After digging around a bit in their answers, I was able to find the most common words and summarize them:

- balanced, invested, eager
- at peace, in the flow, enough
- energized, engaged, passionate
- fun
- influential

We learn from the Golden Circle in Simon Sinek's bestselling book, *Start with Why*, that the limbic brain, responsible for feelings of trust and loyalty and our decision-making, doesn't have the capacity for language.[40] It's no wonder we struggle to describe a great life. When asked to put words to it, the terms are mostly feeling words, and we don't have language that feels tangible like business language for these feelings, so we use metaphors and stories. We're working hard for achievements and success markers that are easy to define but don't fulfill our emotional human needs or tell our story.

Our human needs are personal, emotional, social—and challenging to write on the flip chart into an X to Y goal statement. The promotion, the bonus, or the degree doesn't hit us in the "feels" quite like we thought it would. The celebration of our achievements is often so short that the win never fills the hole, so we look for something new to fill it. We set another achievement goal within minutes after the accomplishments of the day. It's exhausting.

I asked the people who took the survey to mark where they were on average on a zero to one hundred scale, with "burnout" as zero, fifty being "acceptable, no complaints," and one hundred as the "definition of a great life." The result, fifty-seven. Just seven points above "acceptable, no complaints." Even if we're not in a state of burnout, being just "okay" isn't all that inspiring and doesn't have the ability to catapult us into growth. "Okay" doesn't have us jumping out of bed in the morning ready to take on the day. Are we working this hard to be "okay, no complaints"? No wonder we ache, wondering if there is something more. No wonder burnout is a thing. Luckily, most people are still hopeful. I asked if living their description of an extraordinary life is possible at least some of the time; 93 percent said yes. Just 7 percent had given up, lost hope, or never thought it was possible.

Ready for a change, a change that doesn't require you to run away and quit your career? The truth is, we want to work. I once said to a colleague, "I want to be a slacker. Just for a little while. I want to be the one who says, 'Nah, I'm not going in today, just going to hang out.'" He laughed and said, "Rebecca, you'd have a Slacker board of directors created in no time, where you'd organize the slackers for more impactful and valuable slacking." Dammit, he was right. We don't want to "check out"; we want to be passionately engaged in work that matters, work that matters not just to us but also other humans to serve and add value. Work that leaves us with feelings like *energized, eager,* and *influential.* We don't need or want to be slackers; we need connection over control. We need to live and appreciate the rhythm of our lives, the ups and downs of emotion, the joy and the struggle, the story and the money, up and down, ebb and flow. Rhythm says open mind, open heart, open hands.

CHAPTER 13
Ready to Write Your Thrive Story?

Are you ready for your story to honor your sincere desire to work and contribute and not leave you feeling like your well is about to run dry? Pen in hand, engage your Inner Thrive Guide voice; this is your story! Remember the survey I sent out asking professionals what a thriving life was like and if it was possible? They said, "This is hard. I've never really thought about it. I'm not sure what to say." Well, it's time to think about it. It's time to cross that Sea of Uncertainty and engage your Inner Thrive Guide to write your story out of your imagination and your desires.

It's easy to point out what we don't like about our lives. We can look back and see what we wish would have been different in the last hour, last week, or the last decade. We've discussed the work to really know ourselves and to fall in love with our own story; now we tap into our dreams and our intuition. It's time to rise up and out of those old scripts and patterns and write the next chapters of our story, genuinely, authentically.

We can't look to others and emulate their success. Comparison is the thief of joy and innovation. We can learn from, be inspired by, and partner with others, but we don't get to copy and paste their life into ours. Living our lives requires us to live out of our imagination and to set expectations for ourselves. How many holes have we left in the universe by not living our own purpose?

Lindsay Tjepkema, CEO of Casted took the stage in our first Stand Tall in Your Story event on March 5, 2020. Stand Tall in Your Story is a yearly event celebrating the women who have participated in my Rise & Thrive Experience. The title of her talk, "Boldly Be Yourself," depicts the journey of writing her own story and finally living out her unique purpose. Lindsay's mantra, "boldly be yourself" wasn't from some creative vision workshop; this was Lindsay being completely fed up with trying to please everyone else.

Lindsay's story illustrates a lifetime of striving. As a vivacious child, she loved playing dress-up and insisted the family watch her "shows." She was a confident young girl. In school, she was smart and outgoing and loved to learn. This was misinterpreted as too ambitious and too eager. She was told to step back, out of the spotlight. She tried theater to express herself and her vocal talents, but when she didn't get the part, the director said, "I think you probably have the talent, but I don't know, there's just something about you. It's just too much." So Lindsay stepped out of the spotlight and turned down her volume. She tried to be more "likable."

In her first job out of college, her boss was a hard-driving executive who didn't really like Lindsay because she was too young and too kind. To win him over, she overworked, striving and hustling. Her career grew based on this foundation of overworking, which became a problem as she started her family. She doubled down on work to prove that she was serious and ambitious about her career, only to hear from a leader in her company, "You're too cold, abrasive, inflexible, and overly assertive"—this from a fellow mom.

Again, she softened—only to find years later when interviewing for another position a CEO who didn't appreciate this version of Lindsay. He couldn't justify giving some cute girl that kind of salary, the same salary a male counterpart was making. Now, she was too female.

Lindsay realized she was putting her self-worth and personal value entirely into what other people thought she should be, and she was exhausted. She reflected on all she had accomplished with a successful career and raising three young boys, including twins! She realized the only common thread in all of her success was her. So why was she putting so much stake in what other people said and thought of her?

After writing "boldly be yourself" on a blackboard in her kitchen, Lindsay went back to work after the new year. She began to push for her ideas and stand up for her opinions, to listen to her Inner Thrive Guide. Her first success with her new stance of boldly being herself was launching a podcast for her company. Even when leadership pushed back on the idea, she forged ahead, knowing it was a good idea. She then became the host of the podcast where she literally and figuratively found her voice. That podcast led her to leave and start a company of her own, a company focused on ... you guessed it, podcasts. By continuing to follow her Inner Thrive Guide, Lindsay has expanded the company and is launching an entirely new category for business-to-business marketers called Amplified Marketing, and her company is on a rocket ship of growth.

Lindsay's story illustrates that when we walk through life always looking for validation that we're doing it "right," we're striving and actually stifling our growth. Steeped in those education practices of our early years are: get it right, please the teacher, and get good grades. Lindsay spent years looking "out there" for the answers instead of honoring her story at the intersection of her past, present, and her dreams for the future.

Lindsay's story is a very real example of our uniqueness and the personal, emotional, and social aspects of our story. Her story also illustrates the uncertainty each new chapter and stage that growth brings. Lindsay is now a wildly successful CEO leading a company she created from her own experiences, talents, and dreams. Let her story inspire you forward. As her coach, I promise you she still faces uncertainty, especially as a CEO who's creating a new path for marketing and business. She knows how to navigate the Little Bitch in her head, how to surround herself with meaningful connection, and to keep writing her story, chapter by chapter.

We use reflection and connection to honor those things our brain needs to feel a sense of thriving and well-being (*see chart on page 74*).

Personal reflection: look in the mirror and create space and intention for you to take care of you. Nourish to flourish. Our time in reflection determines our level of self-awareness, leading to self-love, self-respect, and self-confidence. This time with ourselves then sets us up for meaningful connections and relationships, both personally and professionally. By investing in and spending time in stillness with ourselves through reflection, we enter into relationships healed and whole. Time spent in personal reflection builds a foundation for our quality of life and career. How much time are you spending in personal reflection now?

I'm going to state it real plain and simple: without the time in reflection to know yourself well, you can't get to thriving. You'll be stuck striving, in a battle with yourself, those old scripts and patterns on repeat. An average person has twelve thousand to sixty thousand thoughts per day, according to the National Science Foundation. Of those, 80 percent are negative and 95 percent are repetitive thoughts.[41] Writing our own story requires the diligence of intentional effort to move past these old negative patterns that keep us striving, struggling, and stuck.

Time in reflection with your Inner Thrive Guide builds a life from your point of view. Without this intense self-awareness, you'll always be at the mercy of repeating the past or living out someone else's opinions and expectations of you.

Here are some journal topics for you. Take them one at a time over a series of days, or take an afternoon to dive into them all. Decide to make these a part of your ongoing routine. For now, just get started; there's no perfect way to dive in. Release the old scripts that are telling you there is a right and a wrong way to do this, and just get curious about you.

Nourish to Flourish: What Feeds Your Soul?

Remember you're writing your story from the depths of your soul, from the bottom of your heart where the love lives. Soul is what makes you *you*. Certain people, places, things, and activities feed your soul and give you joy. What are those things you can do for yourself that feed your soul? This is an important distinction: *what we can do for ourselves.* If you leave these up to the actions of others, you're not writing your own story. If you said, "It feeds my soul when my son calls me from college," it's not that this isn't true, but it illustrates waiting to be fed from someone else. Reflect on the things you can do for yourself. Honestly, I want you to learn how to feel again, deeply and genuinely.

A few of my #SoulFood things are walking in the woods, gathering with a group of friends for dinner and drinks, setting a beautiful table, strolling through a flea market, sniffing a patchouli candle, drinking an amazing oat milk latte, and asking just the right question to help my clients gain clarity in their lives. Too often we bury our #SoulFood under "busy" and abandon the activities that give us joy. When we reintroduce #SoulFood, my clients take dance classes again, start painting again, any of the things they've left behind they can incorporate back into their life.

Take a few minutes and think about your #SoulFood.

SoulFood	
Things	
People	
Activities	
Compliments received	

Receiving compliments is an interesting aspect of #SoulFood. When we receive compliments about who we are more than what we've accomplished, it's a clue to our uniqueness and to those people where we've been relevant, valuable, and making an impact. Too often we've dismissed compliments or questioned them. For a compliment to feed our soul we must choose to receive it. When people thank me for introducing them to a great connection that is helping them in their life or business, that lights up my soul. Connection is one of my superpowers. I feel my best when I've helped someone with connection. When someone reads something I've written and says, "That's exactly what I needed to hear today," it reminds me that I'm using my gift of writing and that I'm listening to the nudges of God and my Inner Thrive Guide working together to bring content that is valuable and relevant in the moment.

Once you know the things that nourish your soul, you can seek them, practice them, participate in them, and feel them nourishing your soul, intentionally.

Feelings Check-In

I learned this simple and profound technique from my friend Kristi Kaiser, a participant of my Rise & Thrive Experience. On a 1-to-10 scale, 1 being the lowest, 10 being the highest, and 5 being neutral, check in periodically by asking yourself or someone else "What's your number"? I assign some symbols to the numbers to truly make it emotional because numbers aren't a story. I'll usually say something like, "On a scale of 1 to 10, with 1 feeling like dog crap on a hot sidewalk, 10 being completely blissed out, and 5 being 'meh,' like the emoji that's all flat eyes and flat mouth, what's your number?"

A few times throughout the week I'll get a text from Kristi, "What's your number?" Simple. It causes me to pause and reflect. How am I feeling? What do I need? What do I want to feel? How can I move myself up the scale or simply sit in the suck for a bit to acknowledge my humanness? In the frenetic pace of our lives, having a regular pause and reflect brings us back to the personal, emotional, and social, reminding us we're not a machine here to produce.

If you're using this with others, here are a couple of quick tips. If someone is a 1 to 3, don't rush into "fixer" mode. Listen and sit with them in the suck. Say things like, "Thank you for sharing that with me. I hate it you're feeling like this." (Anything that says, "I see you.") You may ask, "What would be most helpful for you right now?" The majority of the time, we just want to be seen, heard, and acknowledged for our feelings.

If someone answers they are a 4 to 6, I love to ask, "What could you do to bump up just one number if you wanted to?" They may not want to. But they may need a little inspiration to consider what they could do for themselves.

When someone is a 7 to 10, ask them to tell you about their goodness and their bliss and listen intently, celebrating with them. This wires a memory of goodness into their subconscious they can call upon later. It's impossible to live a 7 to 10 life each and every day. In fact, once we start living more of our best life, we raise the expectations. Writing a thriving story is a growth story, always evolving.

- How do I feel? What's my number?
- How do I want to feel?
- What could I do to move toward the feelings I desire?

Dreams, Our Inner Knowing, the Thrive Guide Specialty

Dreaming is a method to unlocking our uniqueness, the stuff that God wants us to hear but may not be right in front of us. Without dreaming and imagining your best life, you won't attract and recognize the puzzle pieces when they show up. We've fallen prey to a drive-through culture. We've got the ability to have almost everything we need and want delivered through online shopping. But I can't type into a search engine

"Rebecca's best life," order it in my favorite color, and have it delivered the next day.

So much of school and work has been with our faces in a book, in our email, agonizing over the details, working to control every outcome. If thriving is what you're going for, rise up once in a while from the details of the day-to-day to zoom out and think bigger, dream bigger. Our bias for control limits our best life. Zooming out and seeing the bigger picture gets you unstuck far faster than hunkering down managing every detail. You have to look at the front of the puzzle box; you can't just stare at the pieces. Dreaming is designing the picture on the cover of the box.

Rather than critiquing what you like and don't like about the past and the present and looking for more data, more research, more checks off the list, start dreaming about tomorrows. Our story center has a room dedicated to our dreams and hopes for the future. Are you doing your part to fill the dream section of your story center?

All physical creations start with a dream, a vision, an idea. Your dreams are clues to your future. In the frenetic busy of day-to-day life we rarely make enough space for our dreams to lift us up above the fray. We can strategize and plan to make incremental improvements to our life, but to live boldly in our purpose, we need to look at the bigger picture of our story from our dreams.

Dreaming is a verb, an activity, one you do intentionally with grace and space in your life. The Bible says, "Take delight in the Lord, and he will give you the desires of your heart" (Psalm 37:4 NIV). Dreaming is oh so very human, very different than the control, measure, optimizing we've been living for so long. Dreaming has no right and wrong answers. No checklist, no test to pass.

You might ask, "But Rebecca, what if I start dreaming and realize my life sucks?" Great! Awareness is the first step in all change. Let me ask you, "What if you stay stuck in a life that sucks the life out of you or just meander in mediocrity for decades and never give yourself permission to envision anything better?"

And if this question follows, "But what if I dream something so big I can never imagine it would come true?" I hope that's exactly what happens and then you wake up one day realizing God gave you that dream, then he gave you the boldness to take steps toward it and the connections to make it come true. I hope you write me one day and say, "Guess what? My unbelievable bold dream is happening right now!"

What happens in your life if you don't dream? Are you living your life or someone else's? Love yourself enough to dream.

What if ... I wonder if ... Wouldn't it be amazing if ... As you're dreaming, describe what you see, feel, smell, hear, and touch. Describe your feelings. Your brain doesn't know the difference between your dreams and reality. Allowing yourself to dream puts you in the emotional state you desire. When you use your imagination and visualize in great detail, your brain begins to create a memory about that time and space, then logs it into your story center like it's already happened. And as actions and circumstances bring you closer to your dreams, you'll find it a familiar path you'll naturally step into. You're creating it first in your mind, then in real life.

Here's an example of a page in my dream journal: I'm sitting on my enclosed porch looking out over the woods. The Christmas tree lights are flickering, inviting us to the upcoming holiday. My old dogs are at my feet. I love this room. It's all about bringing the outside in. I'm drinking my favorite chai tea from the mug that says *JOY* in beautiful script. I love this mug because I find the joy of this life each day when I wake up. I open my eyes and say, "Thank you, Lord, for another day in this life!" My husband is still sleeping or maybe just pretending to sleep because he knows I cherish the stillness of the morning to capture my thoughts or work on the next book I'm writing. He gets me. He'll rise up soon and we'll get these old dogs to the woods to wander and play.

This is dreaming. I don't have a husband or an enclosed porch—yet. And the holiday season hasn't traditionally been a peachy one for me. I'm dreaming of a time when I've released the past pain and strife of the holidays and replaced it with anticipation. Writing those words gave me peace and joy envisioning the life I dream and desire. Are you ready to grab a journal and a pen and start dreaming? I have a journal dedicated to my dreams. It's fun to go back and see how many have come true.

I have a dream of standing on stage in front of thousands of you who have read this book and started writing your own story. We all come together for you to share your stories with one another. You're thriving, making a difference, living the life of your dreams. The energy in the room is magical. I'm wearing jeans, boots, and a cool jacket with a T-shirt that says "Badass." I'm facilitating a conversation with thousands of you. You're connecting and exchanging info, building real relationships of support with one another.

I have a dream that because we've begun writing our own stories, we want a very different education experience for our children. We've come together to blow up the antiquated education system and build it fresh. We design a system aligned to our brain's natural desire to thrive. Our kids are thriving, the world is changing, we're living the Age of Humanity, no longer treating ourselves as machines here to produce but beautiful humans here to make an impact and serve one another.

Five years ago my dream journal said, "I want to write and speak and help people share their stories." I'm living that dream today, because I had the courage to live out of my imagination.

Before you start, here's a simple ground rule. Let the words and feelings flow: no editing, no grammar checks or second guessing. Get into the flow of writing and writing and writing and see what starts to rise up in you. See what dreams surface and let them see the light of day as you record them on the page. Let your authentic self—your Inner Thrive Guide—lead the way, with no filters and no one's expectations or judgments holding you back. Be bold, be unreasonable, be badass! Pause only to sip your latte or your Manhattan. Let your mind and heart take you on an adventure.

Below are a few prompts to get you started. But this isn't about following the script; it's meant to get your mind wandering so you can follow it around for a while, exploring with wonder and awe, your future life.

- Write a date into the future: five, seven, even ten years into the future.
- It's an ordinary day; where are you? Write like it's a journal entry happening that very moment.
- Describe what's around you. Use details of sights, sounds, smells.
- How are you feeling? Describe the emotions.
- Who is in your life? Describe them and how you're connected.
- Who are you serving and impacting in your life?
- What things are you working on that you're proud of? Excited about?
- What are the things you are grateful for?
- What are the surprises you didn't see coming and are immensely grateful for?

I'm so damn proud of you for dreaming. Seriously, so proud. Now look, I know how this might have gone. You just read the questions and didn't actually do the dreaming. I see you. Is this going to be another one of those books you read, get inspired a little but fall back into old scripts? Are you saying to yourself, *I'll do this later, when I have a new journal or more time?* Great, grab your phone and make an appointment with yourself right now, block it in your calendar. And then once you've done it, make this a part of a regular practice, two or three times per year at a minimum, to check in with your dreams. If you really want to take this seriously, go away by yourself every three to six months on a personal retreat to dream.

So, what's the next chapter? Write the next chapter of your story, not the rest of your story. This distinction makes a significant difference. One chapter at a time. You may be far from living the dream life you've just uncovered. No need to get discouraged; just write the next chapter that will move you closer to those dreams. You don't have to have your whole life figured out. Leave room for the supernatural, the unexpected, the great surprises. In fact, because you dared to dream, God is working to bring all things together for your good, even the stuff that's not in your planner or on your calendar.

We don't acquire our meaning and purpose; we discover it, chapter by chapter. Our life is one big mission, a story we are exploring and writing as we become curious about ourselves. I believe through this process we can use our careers to inform us and guide us to a more meaningful day-to-day life.

Each chapter of our story has meaning and purpose. Spending valuable time in reflection as part of a regular practice aids us to feel the pull to close out a chapter and begin to write a new one or to edit our story. Gaining confidence to navigate the Sea of Uncertainty allows us to introduce bold changes into the rhythm of our lives.

What chapter of your story are you in currently? Is it time to close it out? If so, use these prompts to wrap it up and prepare yourself for the next:

- As I close out this chapter of my story, I am grateful for _____ _____.

- The lessons I'm taking with me are _____ _____.

- What I'm leaving behind is _____ _____.

Like the natural laws of nature, if we are to nourish, we must feed, water, *and* prune. Sometimes we close out chapters and leave things behind to make space for new growth. We may need to leave behind thoughts, fears, things, or people. It's best when we can do this with intention by closing out a chapter.

More than a decade ago I left behind worry. I come from a long lineage of worriers. My mother, her mother, and her mother's mother were all queens of worry and had built castles as an homage to their worry. In my family, worry was synonymous with love. "I'm worried about you" really meant "I love you." To be fair, there were some really shitty experiences that carved patterns of pain deep into their story centers. I saw the toll worry was taking on my mother and grandmother, on their hearts and their bodies. I decided to leave worry behind. When my mother would say, "I'm worried about you," I'd suggest she pray instead of worry and I would assure her I was okay.

Even though my mom thought worry was love, I connected it to guilt. I would feel bad that my mom was worried, so I stopped calling or spending much time with her because I didn't like the way her worrying made me feel. And she wondered how I could love without worry. Was I ignoring how hard things were?

This kept us in a bad cycle. By letting go of the worry, I also had to let go of the guilt. My life didn't take on the generational pattern of worry, and my mom and I got to a better place. Did it happen overnight? No. Is it far better than it was? Absolutely. Sometimes moving into the life we want means leaving things behind.

And I can also hold space for these fine women and the great things they have shown me. I have an antique dish that belonged to my great-grandmother. I use it to hold a bar of Ivory soap in my bathroom. These two things together signify two generations of women in my life. My grandmother bought only Ivory soap, and the smell reminds me of her instantly. She grew up poor but would always say, "You're never too poor to show up clean and neat." There was never a purer relationship in my life than the love from my grandmother. Their strength through adversity and desire to connect and serve reminds me of what I want to continue to emulate, without the worry. Every day at the start of my day, a bar of Ivory soap in an antique dish reminds me to be strong and kind and that these are not mutually exclusive; they're meant to live together as the best representation of humanity.

Name Your Next Chapter

Are you looking to capitalize on what's going well? Are you looking to make dramatic changes? Are you ready for changes that alleviate pain? I find it helpful to name the chapter I'm writing.

Here are some examples:

- Transition—Bigger, Bolder Career Moves
- Surviving Divorce—Better not Bitter
- Parenting Teens—Learning Who They Are Becoming
- On the Path to CEO—What and Whom Do I Need?
- My Nest Isn't Empty, It's Full of You and Me
- Dating—Stepping Up, Stepping Out

You get the idea. What will you call this next chapter you are writing?

Next write a simple story from the title of your chapter: I want to _____ in order to _____ because if I don't _____. Let's use my "Transition—Bigger, Bolder Career Moves" chapter heading as an example. I want to leave my comfort zone and go for a promotion or new projects in order to grow and stretch my skills and abilities because if I don't, I'll become complacent and bored in my life and career. How about "My Nest Isn't Empty, It's Full of You and Me": I want to celebrate what's exciting about the kids going to college in order to explore how much fun I can have with my husband because if I don't, I'll sit in sadness and be no fun for anyone, including myself. This story framework can be immensely helpful in getting started with a new story for any scenario.

CHAPTER 14
Edit Your Story Often

At a time when information is available to us 24/7, our quest to know more and gather more information becomes overwhelming and addictive. Have you ever had an idea and then persuaded yourself to do more research and gather more information, then overcomplicated the idea and ultimately took no action at all? We're obsessed with more. We're not suffering from a lack of information; we're drowning in it.

Human stories are best when they are simple and intentional, breaking things down into the simplest thoughts, ideas, words, and feelings. Humans crave simple human experiences. A great writer benefits from great editing. Our stories are most engaging when we edit often. Let's apply some of our effort and hard work to paring back and simplifying our lives.

We've been gathering information into our brains since we were in the womb. Your story center is amassed with brilliant information and experiences. Conversations, classes, TED Talks, podcasts, books, movies, fights with our parents, squabbles with our spouses—all of these are rich experiences and teachers that aid your life. Simplification is trusting ourselves to have much of the information we need and calling upon it as we need it. Instead of our incessant quest for more, look for ways to pare back, search your own heart, mind, and story center for the answers. Use fewer words, spend less time acquiring, say no to projects and activities, make space to be still, and engage your Inner Thrive Guide, not always another class or degree.

Do Less, Better

The number of things I can accomplish on any given day is freakish. The old me, the striving me would have called it heroic, the stuff of legends. In the midst of a big project, hosting an event, closing a sales gap for the quarter, I'd become a master at the high-stakes tasks game. "Here, hold my beer" kind of epic. Sometimes you need this kind of "roll up your sleeves and get it done" work ethic. Often, though, you don't. Sometimes you need to sit your ass down and think about things for a bit before you take action:

- What is my intent?
- What value or impact am I looking to provide?
- Whom is this for?
- Why does it matter to them?
- Why does it matter to me?
- Should this be delegated to someone else's talents?
- How will this add to my personal story?
- How will this add to the company story?
- How will this impact the money-making model?

I remember the first Christmas I hosted. I love a good party. We were living in the first house we owned, and I was going to rock this thing. I began preparing, creating menus, and setting out all the decorations weeks before the big day. I had worked myself into a tizzy. Checking lists, writing more lists—the more I worked, the more ideas I had to make it better! The night before the big shindig, just before 2 a.m., I was in our dingy basement near tears, rooting through boxes looking for this damn Santa plate. Cussing and frustrated, I stomped up the stairs. My then-husband (this is not why we divorced, by the way) was shutting off the TV and heading to bed. He looked at me and without shouting back said, "You know you're the only one that cares about that damn Santa plate and no one but you will notice it's not there. Go to bed."

Of course he was right. No, I didn't want to hear it. I wanted the damn Santa plate! For the record, I did not go to bed as he suggested. I did keep looking for the plate and finally found it. It added absolutely nothing to the celebration. It did cost me about three hours of sleep and an unnecessary spike in my cortisol level.

As I reflected on this, I had to ask myself, "Who was I doing all this for?" If I'm honest, I was showing off my new house and my mad hosting skills. If I had been thinking more about connecting with my guests and my family, I would have let the Santa plate go and gotten more sleep so I was a more inviting and a well-rested hostess.

It turns out these same ideas apply to your business. The more you try to do, the less you can do with care, concern, empathy, and connection. There's a natural law called the law of diminishing returns. It's as real as the law of cause and effect. You may not like it, but it's true. The more you try to accomplish, the less you can do with meaning, purpose, and authentic connection.

Continually look for things you can stop doing and take off the list of goals for you and your team. Prune, trim, burn it down, celebrate saying no. Remember the staffing company I've referenced? I had taken over a group of offices from an acquisition, and as I was touring the offices and meeting the staff, I noticed a stack of that green-and-white continuous-feed paper we used back in the day with the old dot matrix printers. Four to five inches of that paper was stacked in all the managers' offices, some of it on the corner of the desks, some of it on the floor.

I started asking people what those stacks of reports were. Some gave me a funny look, like "Oh crap, I'm supposed to know, but I don't." Some made up an answer, but none of the answers were consistent. Five offices were physically mailed a large envelope of printed reports monthly. If you stacked all of these together each month, they could have used it for a side table in the reception area. I started thinking about the amount of time and the cost for paper and ink to produce these reports each month that had literally no value because there was no real understanding of what the reports were to be used for. I pictured managers scanning the reports hoping to miraculously uncover information with zero context as to what they were looking for, some feeling embarrassed for not knowing, triggering their overwhelm and uncertainty, assuming they were the only ones who didn't know what to do with them and were too afraid to ask.

I called our corporate office and asked to speak to finance and finally found the person responsible for sending the monthly office report. I don't remember his name, but I do remember the long silence when I asked him to stop running those reports and mailing them to my five branches. He didn't know what their purpose was either. He was following instructions that had been passed to him when someone else had left the department and the roles were divided up among the other staff. He was dutifully checking the box on printing, sorting, and mailing these reports. He was doing a great job; they came out on time each month, and he never missed an office delivery.

After a long silence, he responded, "What will happen if I quit sending them?"

"I don't know, but we're fixin' to find out," I said, spoken in my most authoritative yet kind Midwest redneck speak. As you can imagine, he was concerned. This took a big chunk of his time. He was really wondering if his job was relevant without the hours spent printing, sorting, and mailing those reports.

Guess what happened? Nothing. No consequences, no backlash, nothing. How long had those reports been generated? How many hours spent on nothing? How much shame and frustration from managers wondering what they were supposed to be reading in those reports? How much money spent on paper, ink, and postage?

I'll never know.

What I do know is there are so many things in your life and your work that are just like those reports. Things you do habitually without clarity or context. Things that derive zero value for the time and money spent. But it's not really a zero-sum game; it's taking away time, energy, and effort from the things you could be doing. It's taking away from rest and creative innovation. Create the conditions where people feel safe to ask, "What are these reports for?"—a space where it's okay to ask what feels like a dumb question.

I had some major unwinding to do around this. I have sat in meetings for so many years unintentionally dedicated to overcomplicating things as a leader and a consultant. More info, more data, more research, more value, more service, more of everything in order to show your clients and often our egos that we're smart and worthy. I don't know a single high-achieving badass woman who needs *more*. I personally know hundreds, maybe thousands, who need a nap and a few hours a week to dream about their future and to innovate and create the life of thriving they so desperately deserve. Edit your story often to create space for the main character—you. Edit your story often to clear the clutter that can then elevate the parts of the story that are most intriguing and interesting.

Before you look to another TED Talk, another podcast, another degree, another research report, pause. Take a break from acquiring more and instead listen to your Inner Thrive Guide. She knows. She's freaking fantastic; listen to her.

Maybe you're starting to feel overwhelmed. Maybe you've decided you need to deconstruct your entire life and meticulously evaluate each of the areas in your story's framework. Please don't. Start with this. The one recommendation I can wholeheartedly and boldly recommend for everyone I know is a daily stillness practice. This is how you'll know what to edit, when to close out a chapter, and what new chapter you're beginning.

CHAPTER 15
Let Your Inner Thrive Guide Lead

I know you, I love you, I am you—which means I know those old patterns and scripts are screaming for you to overwhelm yourself with too much and too many expectations, so let me break it down. Don't. Instead, let your Inner Thrive Guide speak each day via a daily stillness practice.

If only I had a dollar for every time a client said to me, "I just need a vacation." Girl, you don't need a vacation; you need a daily stillness practice! Number one, vacations are *not* stress reducing. They are filled with uncertainty and planning and preparation that puts your brain into a stress response even when you're excited to be taking that trip. And number two, if you think taking a break and reducing stress is a biannual occasion, this is a problem.

Let's look at vacations, especially if you have small children or any number of people who are going with you. You're packing up all of their various needs and expectations, which absolutely cannot be met with one trip to the beach or the mountains or anywhere, for that matter.

You spend the week before you leave prepping and planning for every possible scenario that could go wrong at work or at home. You pack for every possible scenario when you arrive on vacation. You shop for two more outfits you don't really need, then moan that you're overpacked. You incessantly check the weather of your destination location. Hell, by the time you get there, your cortisol levels are twice what they are in your day-to-day life, and they were elevated before you started planning this vacation.

Let's reframe the narrative for vacations. Vacations are for exploring, making memories, expanding your experiences so you have new stories in your story center. Yes, depending on your situation, vacations can be very relaxing, but expecting to release stress a few times a year is inadequate. Consider vacation an adventure, not stress relief.

Reducing stress is a daily practice, like food, water, and sleep. A daily stillness practice is a reset for your brain for you to speak to you. I don't care if you have to fake gastrointestinal issues to get away from your kids and take your journal into the bathroom every morning for ten minutes of uninterrupted time. Take your earbuds and drown the kids out with some meditation music. I'm serious; do whatever it takes to spend ten to thirty minutes each day in stillness.

Four years ago, I wrote in my journal, "I just want every morning to feel like Saturday morning." On Saturday mornings I'd take my coffee to the patio and breathe, journal, and pray. I always felt calm and would have the most creative ideas and answers to challenges pop up during those times. I finally realized that I had the power to choose to spend every day with that same stillness. If the benefits were so helpful to my work, why would I *not* do it? My new narrative, this stillness time, is a part of the work, not separate from the work.

I learned from author Eliza Kingsford that we often can't change or eliminate the things that create stress.[42] It's a dicey move to ditch the kids, divorce the husband, and quit your job. So if the stressors are staying in our life, the only thing we can do is take personal responsibility for understanding how to reduce our stress and create stillness. Our lives have been so frenetic for so long that we've normalized stress. We don't even recognize it. Some of us have glamorized stress as a superhero brand. Let that shit go. Nobody looks good in red tights and a cape.

You have certain practices you set up for your business that you don't ignore, like expense reports and paying taxes. Your daily stillness practice is a part of your human needs—just as important as your business practices. Business is human. Just like there are consequences to not doing your taxes, there are consequences to not practicing daily stillness. The need for stillness in thriving is right there with your need for food and water.

Because this is a critical practice, I set up a station with the tools for the job. Just like you have a computer and a phone to do your job, there are tools for the job of a daily stillness practice. I have a stool that serves as a small table sitting beside a chair in front of my sliding glass door out to my patio. On the stool is my journal, a pen, my Bible, and plenty of room for my coffee mug. These are the tools for my daily stillness practice. As I walk through the kitchen to make my morning coffee, I pass this daily stillness practice station. These are the tools to start my day.

Setting up a station and the tools ready for the job is a visual cue that this is a real thing. It also sends a message to your family that it is an important part of your work. Can we please stop apologizing and drop the guilt associated with our work? Our work is a beautiful representation of our gifts and talents. The work we do is helping other humans in some way; it's a part of our story. Sharing the importance of these practices with your loved ones will help them on a path to honor their human needs too.

Set a time and place for your daily stillness practice. When my kids were small, I had three practices I would alternate. I share these because I know kids are the greatest excuse in the world not to do these things, and they are also precisely why you *need* a stillness practice. My three practices were a run, a bubble bath, and a power nap. I'd pick the little angels up from child care, then come home to the witching hour. You know, when the little angels are actually little assholes, including you, everyone tired, hungry, whiny, cranky, and wanting attention.

I explained to my kids that sometimes we need just a few minutes to ourselves to calm our brains before we spend time together. I used SpongeBob SquarePants to help them know how much time we were talking about. One SpongeBob SquarePants episode is eleven minutes; our stillness practices were two SpongeBob SquarePants episodes, twenty-two minutes. I'd make them a snack, turn on SpongeBob SquarePants and do one of my three practices, whichever I needed that day. Then, after twenty-two minutes, I emerged a much better human ready to engage with dinner, conversation, and whatever they needed from me next. Do you have twenty-two minutes to be a better you? Do you have twenty-two minutes to model this for your kids so they can tend to their human needs?

I'm happy to report from setting those expectations and modeling those practices that my kids grew to appreciate and understand how important stillness and rest is for their own well-being. Sometimes after a playdate or a sleepover, my kids would come to me and say, "Can you make them go home now? I need a break." They take their alone time seriously and use it carefully. We are the change makers of the world; let's use our powers for good, really, really good.

Your Weekly Story

To ensure you honor your story and the need for human connection, set a time each week for reflection and connection. As you plan your calendar appointments and tasks for the coming week, look at them and ask:

1. Who is this for? Picture their faces. Do I know them?
2. Why does it matter? To them. To me? What's the human connection of these tasks and appointments? Do I have clarity and context? If not, maybe this should come off my list until I know more.
3. Whom do I need to affirm this week?

Affirmation is different from feedback. We're obsessed with feedback in the business world. The unwritten subtitle of feedback is "Here's what you did wrong." Not all that inspiring. Of course there are situations where feedback is important, such as if you're filling out the wrong forms or not adhering to compliance practices. Affirmation is giving emotional support and encouragement to who someone *is*, not based on what they've accomplished. It sounds something like, "Hey, Holly, I noticed last week when things were really getting heated in the meeting that you stayed really calm and helped people feel heard so we could get to a good place. This is a quality I see in you often. Thank you." Affirmation appeals to our human needs—personal, emotional, and social.

As I look at the tasks to be done and appointments on my calendar, I want to know how the work is affecting other humans, how I can be valuable and relevant. On the first call with the president of my publishing company, I asked her, "Other than liking my book, what would make me a great partner you want to work with? And conversely, what are the behaviors of the authors who are more trouble than they're worth?" I asked the same question with my editor. "How can I make this process better for you?" Business is human. To align our stories, human to human, we ask questions and listen genuinely to how we can serve each other.

Glancing Back

Each week, glance back and journal these things:

1. How did I use my gifts and talents this week?
2. What was the impact?
3. How did it feel?

It's important to remind ourselves of our meaning and purpose weekly, not waiting for accomplishments or performance reviews. With this practice, you'll be pleasantly surprised how valuable and relevant you are to others, even when things are tough.

You may be reading these concepts and thinking, "This is so far from where I'm living now; I don't know where to start." Maybe you feel so stuck in your job that this seems like a foreign language. Please don't wait for the world of work to change before you believe you can change. Our belief we can and should be writing our own story will create this new world of work in our lives. Do it first for yourself and know the rest of us need it too. When we stand tall in our story, we give others courage and confidence to do the same.

I've been fascinated by flash mobs since shortly after Bill Wasik staged the first one in 2003. The idea of this emotional experience from a small group of people dedicated to working together always evoked tears as I watched. Knowing they each had made a commitment, learned their part, and courageously put themselves in a situation to perform with others and among those who were surprised and unaware, I get tears, every time. I'm guessing now that flash mobs evoked this kind of reaction in me because I was witnessing a personal, emotional, and social experience. Human needs met.

I believe this is our flash mob moment to create the Age of Humanity. Maybe, as you commit to reflection with your daily stillness practice, you're learning your own part in this rhythmic dance of life. And as you courageously put yourself out there in connection, you'll be so relevant and impactful that you'll invite others to join you. I invite you to step into the Age of Humanity. It's already begun; now we need your story. We won't change the world with data, facts, and control, but we will change the world with the power of our stories.

Endnotes

1   Kyle Creek (The Captain @sgrstk), "In life, you'll be misunderstood," Twitter, July 9, 2021, https://twitter.com/sgrstk/status/1413677915867209729.

2   Kayley Mulligan, "The Agricultural Revolution," TimeToast, https://www.timetoast.com/timelines/the-agricultural-revolution-6630e11d-055c-4741-befb-12cd0c6c134c.

3   Seth Godin, "Back to (the wrong) school" (PDF), online supplement of Stop Stealing Dreams (What Is School for?) (2012), e-book, 7, https://seths.blog/2011/09/back-to-the-wrong-school/.

4   Alan Deutschman, "Change or Die," *Fast Company*, May 1, 2005, https://www.fastcompany.com/52717/change-or-die.

5   Howard Gardner, *Changing Minds: The Art and Science of Changing Our Own and Other People's Minds* (Boston: Harvard Business School Press, 2004), 82.

6   Harper Douglas, "Etymology of Abundance," Online Etymology Dictionary, https://www.etymonline.com/word/abundance.

7   ——, "Etymology of Rhythm," Online Etymology Dictionary, https://www.etymonline.com/search?q=rhythm.

8   ——, "Etymology of Flourish," Online Etymology Dictionary, https://www.etymonline.com/search?q=flourish.

9   Jonathan Lethem, et al., *Significant Objects: 100 Extraordinary Stories About Ordinary Things* (Seattle: Fantagraphics Books, 2012).

10 Henry IV Parts One and Two, ed. John Crowther (New York: Spark Publishing, 2005), 5.2.81–85. References are to act, scene, and line.

11 Sharon Basaraba, "Increases in Life Span from Prehistory Through the Modern Era," A Guide to Longevity Throughout History, Verywell Health, updated April 23, 2020, https://www.verywellhealth.com/longevity-throughout-history-2224054.

12 Aaron O'Neill, "Life Expectancy of Women at Birth in the United States from 2009 to 2019," International, Statista, September 3, 2021, https://www.statista.com/statistics/263736/life-expectancy-of-women-in-the-united-states/.

13 Amy Blaschka, "Everything You've Ever Wanted Is Sitting on the Other Side of Fear," *Forbes*, September 4, 2018, https://www.forbes.com/sites/amyblaschka/2018/09/04/everything-youve-ever-wanted-is-sitting-on-the-other-side-of-fear/?sh=1a2463613979.

14 Rebecca Fleetwood Hession, "90 Seconds to a Life You Love with Dr. Joan Rosenberg PhD – Part 2," May 27, 2019, *The Badass Women's Council*, podcast, 11:48, https://listen.casted.us/public/18/The-Badass-Womens-Council-bdcba16b/bc24a92b.

15 Harper Douglas, "Etymology of Normal," Online Etymology Dictionary, https://www.etymonline.com/search?q=normal.

16 Rebecca Fleetwood Hession, "The Regenerative Life with Carol Sanford," March 27, 2020, *The Badass Women's Council*, podcast, 49:37, https://listen.casted.us/public/18/The-Badass-Womens-Council-bdcba16b/85562e0e.

17 Matthew Lieberman, *Social: Why Our Brains Are Wired to Connect* (New York: Crown Publishers, 2013).

18 ——, "The Social Brain and Its Superpowers," October 7, 2013, TEDx Talk, MP3 audio, 17:58, https://singjupost.b-cdn.net/wp-content/uploads/2016/10/The-social-brain-and-its-superpowers-by-Matthew-Lieberman-Ph.D.-at-TEDxStLouis-2013.mp3.

19 Cigna, *Cigna US Loneliness Index: Survey of 20,000 Americans Examining Behaviors Driving Loneliness in the United States* (PDF), May 2018, 2, https://www.cigna.com/assets/docs/newsroom/loneliness-survey-2018-updated-fact-sheet.pdf.

20 Rebecca Fleetwood Hession, "Thriving: Business Owner x 2, Wife and Toddler Mom," January 17, 2021, *The Badass Women's Council*, podcast, 35:01, https://listen.casted.us/public/18/The-Badass-Womens-Council-bdcba16b/41a0e682.

21 "The Morning Show," season 1, episode 1, "In the Dark Night of the Soul It's Always 3:30 in the Morning," directed by Mimi Leder, written by Kerry Ehrin and Jay Carson, aired November 1, 2019, on Apple+ TV, https://tv.apple.com/us/show/the-morning-show/umc.cmc.25tn3v8ku4b39tr6ccgb8nl6m.

22 Daniel H. Pink, *Drive: The Surprising Truth About What Motivates Us* (New York: Riverhead Books, 2009).

23 Amy C. Edmondson, *The Fearless Organization: Creating Psychological Safety in the Workplace for Learning, Innovation and Growth* (Hoboken: Wiley, 2018).

24 Dustin Siggins, "3 Mistakes Sherwin-Williams Made in Firing TikTok Star Tony Piloseno," *PR Daily*, December 3, 2020, https://www.prdaily.com/3-mistakes-sherwin-williams-made-in-firing-tiktok-star-tony-piloseno/.

25 Adam Gale, "Why Amazon Banned PowerPoint," *Management Today*, July 15, 2020, https://www.managementtoday.co.uk/why-amazon-banned-powerpoint/leadership-lessons/article/1689543.

26 Emma Green, "The Origins of Office Speak," *The Atlantic*, April 24, 2014, https://www.theatlantic.com/business/archive/2014/04/business-speak/361135/.

27 F. John Reh, "What the Phrase 'Boil the Ocean' Means in Business," Management Skills, The Balance Careers, updated November 14, 2019, https://www.thebalancecareers.com/the-meaning-of-odd-business-phrases-boil-the-ocean-2276187.

28 Harper Douglas, "Etymology of Context," Online Etymology Dictionary, https://www.etymonline.com/word/context.

29 Marsha Sinetar, *Do What You Love, the Money Will Follow: Discovering Your Right Livelihood* (New York: Dell Publishing, 1987).

30 Chris McChesney, Sean Covey, and Jim Huling, *The 4 Disciplines of Execution: Achieving Your Wildly Important Goals* (New York: Free Press, 2012).

31 Harper Douglas, "Etymology of Prosper," Online Etymology Dictionary, https://www.etymonline.com/word/prosper#etymonline_v_2718.

32 JoLynne Whittaker Ministries, "FINANCIAL PROSPERITY IS OF GOD!" Facebook, February 3, 2019, https://www.facebook.com/ProphetJoLynne/photos/financial-prosperity-is-of-god-thats-a-word-for-all-the-people-who-believe-chris/2200926229946197/.

33 Shawn Achor, *The Happiness Advantage: The Seven Principles of Positive Psychology That Fuel Success and Performance at Work* (New York: Crown Business, 2010).

34 Godin, "Back to (the wrong) school."

35 Tom McArthur, *Learning Rhythm and Stress*, (Glasgow: Collins, 1978).

36 Anand Venkataraman, Heather Balance, and John B. Hogenesch, "The Role of the Circadian System in Homeostasis," chap. 21 in *Handbook of Systems Biology* (Cambridge: Academic Press, 2013), 407.

37 Michael Rosbash, "Department of Biology," Faculty, Brandeis University, https://www.brandeis.edu/biology/faculty/rosbash-michael.html.

38 John Haltiwanger, "Optimistic People All Have One Thing in Common: They're Always Late," *Elite Daily*, June 30, 2015, https://www.elitedaily.com/life/culture/optimistic-people-have-one-thing-common-always-late/1097735.

39 Laura Shocker, "This Is Why You're Late All the Time (and What to Do About It)," *HuffPost* (blog), November 7, 2013, 8:48 a.m., EST, https://www.huffpost.com/entry/psychology-lateness_n_4229057.

40 Simon Sinek, *Start with Why: How Great Leaders Inspire Everyone to Take Action* (New York: Portfolio, 2009).

41 Nergina Antanaityte, "Mind Matters: How to Effortlessly Have More Positive Thoughts," TLEX (blog), https://tlexinstitute.com/how-to-effortlessly-have-more-positive-thoughts/.

42 Eliza Kingsford, "Health & Weight Loss Psychotherapist," November 2, 2021, https://www.elizakingsford.com/.

Bibliography

Achor, Shawn. *The Happiness Advantage: The Seven Principles of Positive Psychology That Fuel Success and Performance at Work*. New York: Crown Business, 2010.

Antanaityte, Nergina. "Mind Matters: How to Effortlessly Have More Positive Thoughts." TLEX (blog). https://tlexinstitute.com/how-to-effortlessly-have-more-positive-thoughts/.

Basaraba, Sharon. "Increases in Life Span from Prehistory Through the Modern Era." A Guide to Longevity Throughout History. Verywell Health. Updated April 23, 2020. https://www.verywellhealth.com/longevity-throughout-history-2224054.

Blaschka, Amy. "Everything You've Ever Wanted Is Sitting on the Other Side of Fear." *Forbes*, September 4, 2018. https://www.forbes.com/sites/amyblaschka/2018/09/04/everything-youve-ever-wanted-is-sitting-on-the-other-side-of-fear/?sh=1a2463613979.

Cigna. *Cigna US Loneliness Index: Survey of 20,000 Americans Examining Behaviors Driving Loneliness in the United States* (PDF). May 2018, 2. https://www.cigna.com/assets/docs/newsroom/loneliness-survey-2018-updated-fact-sheet.pdf.

Creek, Kyle (The Captain @sgrstk). "In life, you'll be misunderstood." Twitter. July 9, 2021. https://twitter.com/sgrstk/status/1413677915867209729.

Deutschman, Alan. "Change or Die." *Fast Company*. May 1, 2005. https://www.fastcompany.com/52717/change-or-die.

Douglas, Harper. "Etymology of Abundance." Online Etymology Dictionary. https://www.etymonline.com/word/abundance.

——. "Etymology of Context." Online Etymology Dictionary. https://www.etymonline.com/word/context.

——. "Etymology of Flourish." Online Etymology Dictionary. https://www.etymonline.com/search?q=flourish.

——. "Etymology of Normal." Online Etymology Dictionary. https://www.etymonline.com/word/normal.

——. "Etymology of Prosper." Online Etymology Dictionary. https://www.etymonline.com/search?q=normal.

——. "Etymology of Rhythm." Online Etymology Dictionary. https://www.etymonline.com/search?q=rhythm.

Edmondson, Amy C. *The Fearless Organization: Creating Psychological Safety in the Workplace for Learning, Innovation and Growth.* Hoboken: Wiley, 2018.

Gale, Adam. "Why Amazon Banned PowerPoint." *Management Today.* July 15, 2020. https://www.managementtoday.co.uk/why-amazon-banned-powerpoint/leadership-lessons/article/1689543.

Gardner, Howard. *Changing Minds: The Art and Science of Changing Our Own and Other People's Minds.* Boston: Harvard Business School Press, 2004. 82.

Godin, Seth. "Back to (the wrong) school" (PDF). Online supplement of *Stop Stealing Dreams (What Is School for?).* 2012. E-book. 7. https://seths.blog/2011/09/back-to-the-wrong-school/.

Green, Emma. "The Origins of Office Speak." *The Atlantic.* April 24, 2014. https://www.theatlantic.com/business/archive/2014/04/business-speak/361135/.

Haltiwanger, John. "Optimistic People All Have One Thing in Common: They're Always Late." *Elite Daily.* June 30, 2015. https://www.elitedaily.com/life/culture/optimistic-people-have-one-thing-common-always-late/1097735.

Hession, Rebecca Fleetwood. "90 Seconds to a Life You Love with Dr. Joan Rosenberg PhD – Part 2." May 27, 2019. *The Badass Women's Council.* Podcast, 11:48. https://listen.casted.us/public/18/The-Badass-Womens-Council-bdcba16b/bc24a92b.

———. "The Regenerative Life with Carol Sanford." March 27, 2020. *The Badass Women's Council.* Podcast, 49:37. https://listen.casted.us/public/18/The-Badass-Womens-Council-bdcba16b/85562e0e.

———. "Thriving: Business Owner x 2, Wife and Toddler Mom." January 17, 2021. *The Badass Women's Council.* Podcast, 35:01. https://listen.casted.us/public/18/The-Badass-Womens-Council-bdcba16b/41a0e682.

JoLynne Whittaker Ministries. "FINANCIAL PROSPERITY IS OF GOD!" Facebook. February 3, 2019. https://www.facebook.com/ProphetJoLynne/photos/financial-prosperity-is-of-god-thats-a-word-for-all-the-people-who-believe-chris/2200926229946197/.

Kingsford, Eliza. "Health & Weight Loss Psychotherapist." November 2, 2021. https:// www.elizakingsford.com/.

Leder, Mimi, dir. *The Morning Show.* Season 1, episode 1. "In the Dark Night of the Soul It's Always 3:30 in the Morning." Aired November 1, 2019, on Apple+ TV. https://tv.apple.com/us/show/the-morning-show/umc.cmc.25tn3v8ku4b39tr6ccgb8nl6m.

Lieberman, Matthew. "The Social Brain and Its Superpowers." October 7, 2013. TedX Talk. YouTube, 17:58. https://www.youtube.com/watch?v=NNhk3owF7RQ.

———. *Social: Why Our Brains Are Wired to Connect.* New York: Crown Publishers, 2013.

McArthur, Tom. *Learning Rhythm and Stress.* Glasgow: Collins, 1978.

McChesney, Chris, Sean Covey, and Jim Huling. *The 4 Disciplines of Execution: Achieving Your Wildly Important Goals.* New York: Free Press, 2012.

Mulligan, Kayley. "The Agricultural Revolution." TimeToast. https://www.timetoast.com/timelines/the-agricultural-revolution-6630e11d-055c-4741-befb-12cd0c6c134c.

O'Neill, Aaron. "Life Expectancy of Women at Birth in the United States from 2009 to 2019." International. Statista. September 3, 2021. https://www.statista.com/statistics/263736/life-expectancy-of-women-in-the-united-states/.

Pink, Daniel H. *Drive: The Surprising Truth About What Motivates Us.* New York: Riverhead Books, 2009.

Reh, F. John. "What the Phrase 'Boil the Ocean' Means in Business." Management Skills. The Balance Careers. Updated November 14, 2019. https://www.thebalancecareers.com/the-meaning-of-odd-business-phrases-boil-the-ocean-2276187.

Rosbash, Michael. "Department of Biology." Faculty. Brandeis University. https://www.brandeis.edu/biology/faculty/rosbash-michael.html.

Shakespeare, William. *Henry IV Parts One and Two.* Edited by John Crowther. New York: Spark Publishing, 2005. 5.2.81–85. References are to act, scene, and line.

Shocker, Laura. "This Is Why You're Late All the Time (and What to Do About It)." *HuffPost* (blog). November 7, 2013. 8:48 a.m., EST. https://www.huffpost.com/entry/psychology-lateness_n_4229057.

Siggins, Dustin. "3 Mistakes Sherwin-Williams Made in Firing TikTok Star Tony Piloseno." *PR Daily.* December 3, 2020. https://www.prdaily.com/3-mistakes-sherwin-williams-made-in-firing-tiktok-star-tony-piloseno/.

Sinek, Simon. *Start with Why: How Great Leaders Inspire Everyone to Take Action.* New York: Portfolio, 2009.

Sinetar, Marsha. *Do What You Love, the Money Will Follow: Discovering Your Right Livelihood.* New York: Dell Publishing, 1987.

Sittenfeld, Curtis, Ben Greenman, Mattew De Abaitua, Rob Agredo, Blake Butler, Matthew Sharpe, Susannah Breslin, et al. *Significant Objects: 100 Extraordinary Stories About Ordinary Things.* Seattle: Fantagraphics Books, 2012.

Venkataraman, Anand, Heather Balance, and John B. Hogenesch. "The Role of the Circadian System in Homeostasis." Chap. 21 in *Handbook of Systems Biology.* Cambridge: Academic Press, 2013. 407.

World Health Organization. "Burn-out an 'Occupational Phenomenon': International classification of Diseases." Departmental News. World Health Organization. May 28, 2019. https://www.who.int/news/item/28-05-2019-burn-out-an-occupational-phenomenon-international-classification-of-diseases.

——. "Mental Health in the Workplace." Mental Health and Substance Use. World Health Organization. https://www.who.int/teams/mental-health-and-substance-use/promotion-prevention/mental-health-in-the-workplace.

Acknowledgments

To my parents, Ron and Connie Fleetwood, for trusting me to be curious to explore my own story. Thank you for not saddling me with expectations of achievement, instead only inspiring me to be a good human and loving me through the rough spots, like that little Daytona Beach runaway chapter as just one example of where my curiosity took me.

To my kids, Cameron and Auburn, for choosing to be good humans. I'm ridiculously proud to be your mom. I had no idea this book would take me three years to write. I know this was often a great distraction in our lives. You comforted me and inspired me to keep going. And … you bought and made your own food, a lot. I promise to sell enough copies to take us on a nice trip to make it up to you. Let this book be your permission to explore and write your own story, always.

To the original Badass Women's Council: Alex Perry, Jennifer Robbins, Nicole Busch, Lindsay Boccardo, Erin Fischer, and Emily Sutherland. Thank you for jumping into a grand experiment and bringing your whole self on the journey. We've all grown and evolved since that first Café Patachou meeting. Your courage to jump in was what enabled the brand to take on a life of its own, and I'm immensely grateful. You never forget your first. Wink, wink.

And to you, specifically, Alex Perry, for your laughter, prayers, tears, and ruthless authenticity for an entire year over Voxer messaging while I sat on my patio and finished this beast. You kept me upright.

To Scott Miller for checking in regularly. Your messages always seemed to come at just the right time. You had no intent other than to inspire a fellow writer and friend. I felt seen, and I won't forget it.

To the participants of Rise and Thrive Season 1; Courtney Simpkiss, Amber Fields, Wendy Noe, Kelly Wingham, Lindsay Tjepkema and Denisa Lambert for jumping into another of my grand experiments. I don't think I've ever felt more vulnerable crossing the Sea of Uncertainty. Not only were you willing participants, but you were also holding me up as we crossed that sea together. Watching you take the stage for the first Stand Tall in Your Story event was an out-of-body experience, watching a dream come to life.

And to the Bible and bourbon for always being by my side. To Jesus for downloading the ideas for these grand experiments, and to a great Manhattan to see it through those oh-shit-what-have-I-done days and in grand celebration. Dear Jesus, keep those ideas coming.

Victoria -
Rebecca is a perfect match
for a keynote, team development
or an empowerment series
for 2023. We have you covered
with content and programming
for your team.

All best,
Jacque O